Footsteps in the West

Footsteps in the West

Satish Desai, OBE

Produced and published by
Whittles Publishing Services
Roseleigh House,
Latheronwheel,
Caithness, KW5 6DW,
Scotland, UK

ISBN 1-870325-93-1

Printed by
J.W.Arrowsmith Ltd.,
Bristol

Sponsored by
**CROYDON
COUNCIL**

Contents

To My Mother
Lilabai Desai

Acknowledgements

I am grateful to my friends for their encouragement and help in writing this book, especially Carol West and Yeshwant Mali. Carol has read the earlier versions of my book and made useful suggestions. Yeshwant Mali, a renowned artist and my friend for the past thirty years, has drawn the sketches based on some photographs but mainly with the help of his imagination.

I wish to thank the Croydon Council for their sponsorship of the publication of this book. Among the officials at the Croydon Council, Adrienne Bloch (the Heritage Development Officer) has been very supportive of this project. I have always admired Krishna Ray, the Ethnic Minority Information Officer, as an accomplished singer and exponent of Indian classical music. I am grateful to her for encouraging local writers and artists to present their works at functions arranged by her at Croydon.

My family and I have lived happily in Croydon for the last seventeen years. We have taken part in the social and educational activities here, including service on Governing Bodies by my wife and me at Priory School and Atwood School respectively. I wish to repay my debt to Croydon, albeit in a modest way, in the form of my book about experiences in life elsewhere in the world. I hope that it will be of interest to all people here, particularly the younger generation, irrespective of their origin and their background.

Preface

*I*t used to be a pastime for grandparents and parents at one time, to tell stories to the youngsters about their experience in life. With the changes in culture nowadays, the youngsters have more important things on their minds and the adults also may not have the time to spare. I am not sure whether I could tell my stories to my grandchildren, as I haven't been so fortunate to have any so far. Even if they do come along in good time, I am not sure whether they will wish to listen to my past. Nevertheless, they should have some way to know, if they wished to know, how I came to be in the West from where I had started my life in the East. I also hope that my stories may interest other youngsters and not only my own grandchildren. I have, therefore, thought of writing them down and I have managed to find some time to do so.

I have lived in two different worlds and two different times. I grew up in India and lived there for the first twenty-eight years. I then came to the UK and I have been here for the last thirty years. I came here to work as a civil engineer, the only profession I really cared to pursue. I did not come here for advanced studies or to make any point or to represent anything. My narrations in this book concern people I met and their influence on me, during my time in India and during the period when I made my home in the West. My early days in the UK were like landing on a planet with different gravity and atmosphere. It was, therefore, not easy to walk steadily straight away. Every child learns to walk, with the help of its parents but mostly learning on its own with a stumble or two in the beginning. In the same way, every child becomes a young person and comes to term with the adult world, step by step and mostly on its own, unless the parents have provided a protected passage for him or her, clear of all obstacles. I had this experience twice, once in Mumbai as a youngster and, as an adult, when I learnt my footsteps in the West. The later part of my life in the

West has also been quite eventful, not strictly as planned or not all with sugar and spice. But it is continuing and it is not quite the right time to tell anyone about it.

In my younger days, I did not understand why some things happened the way they did. However, I do not understand them even today, perhaps, because they have changed and I have changed a little as well.

My early difficulties started when I learnt to multiply and divide. I could not divide one by zero. My teacher told me to stop being silly. The poor man did not have an answer. My next stop was geography and I wished to know how and when the sun and the stars came in existence. Could the planets and stars have any influence on human life? There were no answers to this either. My mother, a life-long primary teacher, mentioned the name God and the Hindu concept of Trinity. The God as Brahma has created the universe, as Vishnu He will look after it and as Mahesh (Shankara) He will end it when the time comes. At the beginning of life on earth, there was a story about Manu, who was the first human being. The word "Manushya" or "Man" came from his name "Manu". He was supposed to have been stranded on the top of a mountain during a very large flood, which destroyed all creatures except a few. Manu had a boat, in which he kept these fortunate creatures. In the end, a big fish with a horn came to Manu's rescue and he could tie a rope round the horn. Manu was taken to safety and the life on earth redeveloped thereafter, all over again. It seemed to be rather unreal and I lost my faith in what the religious books seemed to say. Could there be so much that we shall never know and not understand? This seemed a fair thought. Could human knowledge have to be something conditional and within limits and should we push out to the God's regime all that we cannot understand? This seemed temporarily satisfactory and gave me the first concept of God. To my mother's relief, I carried on studying.

Besides the lack of understanding of the past, a few things seemed impossible for me to understand, although they existed. Light could be made of either particles or waves, since its structure would be destroyed as one tried to get too close to examine it with the current techniques. But surely, we are not going to give up and we shall keep trying to search for answers. This gave me the second concept of the God as the provider of correct direction, although the distance between the truth and human understanding is too large to be bridged for the time being. The Indian scripture, Geeta, quotes the God as saying something similar, "Remember me and compete."

The next conflict arose from reading Geeta itself. Whom do I compete with? At school, it was fair enough to start with. One worked hard and got to the top of the class, which would not hurt anyone else. Even this was not quite true. At one stage, I came first, ahead of another boy who was expected to do so all the time. He was really a gem of a fellow. When we came back from summer holidays to the higher standard, he was not there. I learnt that he could not receive support from the charity that had helped him until then, since he had lost his top position. The boy ran away to study at Kashi in north India. I was miserable for some time until I knew that he was admitted in a sanctuary for bright people. I met him after some fifteen years, when he had passed a degree in law. All had ended well!

Is the locality the unit for brotherhood of men and should men not travel and meet other tribes at all, for the fear that they would start fighting? What about the Europeans who took over America from the natives and took millions of Africans as slaves, to create a powerful and prosperous nation? It all seems obviously unfair, except when one compares the state of black Americans with the fate of those seen starving and killing each other in Africa.

I often wondered why millions of Indians could not overcome the British and avoid loss of independence for 150 years. I think that people were not aware of the nationhood as such. They accepted what came in place of the anarchy that existed locally in many parts of India during the middle of nineteenth century. Not until the early twentieth century did some leaders like Tilak succeed in putting some life in the cold mass of people in India. As a youngster, I did not think much of my ancestors, who fought among each other and surrendered to the outsiders. Some pundits even invented references in some old religious scriptures and suggested that they included a prediction about the coming of British Raj as inevitable and good for India!

Such instances bring out the shortcomings of the general concept of a religion. It seems that the God's messenger establishes a religion or His appearance rectifies the balance in favour of the righteous from time to time, as Hindus believe. Most religions have the same basic principles giving the same direction towards righteousness. But the human race is unable to follow the direction in a straight line for very long. Instead, the line curves away from the original direction, under the influence of greed of the powerful and rich, and the prescriptive doctrines develop. Science, even with its limited scope, has provided strength to some men of vision to stand up against the aberrations and philosophy has often been the inspiration for the scientists. In early seventeenth century, Galileo Galilei stood up against the Church to speak out that the earth revolved round the sun and lost his freedom for eight years, for being the "heretic astronomer". He was luckier than Giordano Bruno of the sixteenth century, who was burnt alive in Rome for refusing to deny that the God existed in nature.

(I was delighted to read in October 1998, that the Pope used Galileo's writing to support his own pronouncements in his 13th encyclical *"Fides et Ratio"*, which had the link between faith and reason as its main theme.)

Being aware of my limitations to investigate the causes of such deviations of people from the true path all over the world, I wondered if I should look at my birthplace more closely. Memories soon came back about the recent past. I also remembered some stories about my ancestors and the olden times, more fictional than historical records. I decided to put the memories of characters and thoughts together in some order. My intention was to see if any pattern could emerge and a model could be constructed, in a limited sense, based on the understanding of past and present development of a local society and my own experience in the new world.

In my narratives, I have remained faithful to the events, as far as possible, as they happened around me and as I remember them. In the interest of story-telling, however, I have filled in a few gaps with my imagination and mixed and merged the real-life characters to such an extent that the emerging ones have nearly become fictional. I would also like to say that I have not deliberately criticised anyone or any ideology. I have written what seemed appropriate to me, based on my perception of what I could remember and discover. I hope that it is entertaining and it is adequate to form a picture of the things as they were in Mumbai in early days and the process leading up to my footsteps in the West. Perhaps I could come back and have another word with the readers in the Epilogue, after I have finished the narratives!

1
The Background

*I*ndia is a mixture of many different cultures, showing various shades of Hinduism with local influence from place to place. The variations also suit the pantheist principles of the religion. God is seen and worshipped in many forms, ranging from romantic Shrikrishna in Gujarat to the fierce image of Shankara or even goddess Kali elsewhere. The basic religion has its origin in the Aryan scriptures like the Vedas. Aryans came to India through Kashmir before 1800 B.C. and colonised the fertile region on the banks of the river Ganga. (This original name of the river is commonly mispronounced and spelt as Ganges.)

The religion was soon localised, introducing the importance of farming and realising that the cow was too useful an animal to be killed for meat. Traditions of the indigenous people were absorbed gradually by the developing civilisation. As far as possible, the developing religion adopted rituals like worshipping trees, stones and animals. On the other hand, stories in some epics suggest that the stubborn and non-compliant tribes could well have been ruthlessly eliminated, for example, Mahabharata, one of the two best-loved epics (the other being Ramayana). It includes a record that Lord Krishna and his devotee and friend Arjuna burnt down an entire region called Khandavavana. They wanted to destroy the tribe called Nagas (snakes in Sanskrit) that lived there. They guarded the region with the help of armed soldiers and deadly weapons to ensure that no one should escape. Some did escape, however, and survived to kill the young princes in Arjuna's family later on as a revenge, but that is another story. This shows that all was not fair with the warriors and politicians even in the prehistoric times. However, questioning historical acts is often futile, since the history only gives an account of the events. The original Sanskrit word Itihas gives this meaning, when it is deciphered as "Iti ha aas" or "so it was".

The spread of religion to the South had come about with the journey of Rama, the prince of Ayodhya in north India, as described in the epic

Ramayana, which preceded Mahabharata. Rama was exiled by his father, under the influence of Rama's stepmother, who wanted her own son to be the king in place of Rama. Rama left with his wife Seeta and his brother and travelled to the South, crossing the central Indian mountain range called the Vindhya Parvata. This range was quite impassable at that time. (Even during the British Raj, it was known to be the most difficult terrain, notorious for the Thagis, the notorious robbers.) Rama established friendship with the southern people referred to as Monkeys in the story, who helped him to win the war against the Shrilankan king, the villain Ravana. Seeta was kidnapped by this villain, who was a powerful ruler and a great warrior. However, these so-called monkeys were able to build a bridge between the southern-most tip of India (Rameshwara) and Shrilanka, which was vital for the allied victory. In addition to its value as a religious book, Ramayana is a significant record of the early influence of northern civilisation on south India, albeit with some poetic licence and subsequent additions over so many years.

Centuries passed after the journey of Rama but the differences between the descendants of the people from the North and the indigenous southerners remained largely as they were. The developing caste system included many dark-coloured southern tribes as servants or Shudras, unlike those found in the North by the Aryans in previous centuries. The descendants of the fair-skinned northerners were Kshatriyas (warriors), Brahmins (intellectual priests and teachers) and Vaishyas (tradesmen and farmers). Shivaji Raja, who fought the Mughals and established a free Hindu state in the South in the seventeenth century, was a Kshatriya and proud of his origin. Maharashtra was the name given to the province established by Shivaji. The language Marathi was derived from Sanskrit and developed and enriched by scholars and poets, to take the literature to the common people.

The earlier part my story follows loosely the lives of some characters from my community. The history of our community goes back to some three hundred years before Shivaji's times. I understand that the community originated in the north Indian region called Rajputana. This region is the homeland of Rajpoots who are believed to be the direct descendants of Aryans. Rajpoot literally means descendant of a king. In one of the states of Rajputana, a king called Bimba Raja ruled very happily until one of his sons stepped out of line and lost the king's favour. Such things were quite common in royal families but, unfortunately, the differences could not be resolved and the king promptly extradited the prince and some two thousand of his supporters. The prince must have done something really wrong, since none of the other kings would accept him in their states. The hapless young man had to move southwards, facing all the hazards of a journey through the unknown. He somehow crossed the Vindhya mountain range and reached the region around Mumbai or Bombay as it was called until recently. His bravery and the loyal support of his followers enabled him to develop some barren land. His subjects started growing crops and built houses, pursuing the skills inherited from their ancestors.

The fledgling little kingdom prospered and the prince established a good rapport with the native tribe of fishermen. His followers had good craftsmen among them, carpenters and sculptors, who made good use of the timber from the rich forest and the granite from the mountains to construct temples and monuments. The fishermen soon started to admire the skills of the settlers, who diversified their carpentry skills in ship-building to the delight of the fishermen. The newcomers had never seen the ocean before but they were capable of working out the ways of building vessels with provisions required to make them stable and manoeuvrable. The fishermen themselves were very agile, athletic, and expert mariners. The settlers adapted to the diet of fish and rice and the cuisine that made generous use of coconuts. These items were plentiful and the local tribes supplied them fresh, with a barter system that worked well. All the people lived in harmony and prospered.

The prince became very close to the tribal chief and his family, the charming princes and princesses and the affectionate elders. As the friendship grew, the chief revealed his feelings to the prince one day, about the lowly status given to him by the old Hindu priests. These priests were descendants of the wise men who had stayed behind at the time of Ramayana. The fishermen had become Hindus and they provided food, protection from bandits and all possible help to the Ashramas or sanctuaries, where the elders prayed and taught the youngsters. The priests were not racists by nature but they believed so strongly in the religious books that they could not do anything that was not given in the scriptures. Naturally, the books had no provision for giving recognition to the fishermen for their skills and expertise in maritime activities and make them Kshatriyas.

Within a few years, a disaster struck the little state. Pirates from other coastal regions came to know about the new settlers and they attacked, looted the farm produce at night-time and fled with their ships before dawn. The prince was helpless. Although the pirates would not come every year, their first attack left bad scars on the pride of the prince as an invincible warrior and his people suffered from a severe loss of morale.

A solution was soon found by the two leaders, the chief and the prince. The crafts were fitted with weapons and both sides trained together for watching and defending the villages and farms against any future pirate attack. The preparation was to be put to test soon, when the vigilant fishermen reported sighting of pirate ships. The allied fighting forces got ready for a new and exciting experience for both sides. The priests dithered a little to start with, since they knew only the way to bless the combatants on land, horsemen and soldiers. They had no experience of blessing the navy but they soon adopted the old verses for the new task of providing the sea-going warriors with heavenly support. The allies fought a fierce battle against the experienced pirates. The new alliance of the prince and the chief finally won against all the odds. It was the beginning of a new era.

Quite naturally, the fishermen had acquitted themselves well as worthy warriors. They had proved themselves to be tough, disciplined and courageous, which were the acknowledged qualities of true Kshatriyas. The prince met the priests and let them know his momentous decision. He would marry the daughter of the fishermen's chief! He asked the priests to perform the ceremony and accept the king and fishermen as Kshatriyas. The priests grudgingly complied with the prince's plans and the religious rules were rewritten with the help of the wise elders.

Pirates did not come back but the fishermen and settlers prospered and strengthened the bond between families with blood relations. This was the birth of the community of my ancestors. The following generations succeeded in ramping up their achievements with combination of skills inherited from both sides of their ancestors. They moved closer to the coast and occupied seven islands, called the "Islands of Mumbai". (This name has its origin in the temple of Goddess Mumbai or Mumbadevi, known as a version of Laxmi, the goddess of wealth.) The islands were separated during the high tide only and one could walk from one island to the other, when the tide was low enough.

Ultimately, a part of the West Coast of India near Mumbai was colonised by the Portuguese after the visit of Vasco de Gama in 1498. My ancestors fought bravely against the invaders but they could not match the Europeans armed with advanced weapons. Another twist in the history came in the form of a wedding. The daughter of King John IV of Portugal, Catherine of Braganza, married the Merry Monarch Charles II of Great Britain and Ireland in 1662. The King gave his daughter away with a generous dowry, including valuable trading privileges and port cities of Tangier (Morocco) and Mumbai. In return, England pledged to help Portugal maintain its independence from Spain. It is ironic that the arranged marriage and the dowry should be similar to the traditions prevalent in Mumbai, which might have influenced the married life of Catherine like a daughter of a rich man from Mumbai. In spite of the generosity of her father, she had some hard time with her brother-in-law (James, the duke of York), who accused her of trying to poison the King and wanted the King to divorce her. An Indian daughter-in law would have known the feeling! Charles II stood by his wife, however, and she helped in his conversion to the Roman Catholic Church. This would also appear to be characteristically similar to the good old Indian ladies, whose love for their religion was far stronger than that of the contemporary men.

The shallow sea and marshes were filled up to form a single island of Mumbai later on. The indigenous community prospered under the British, with their skills adapted to the European style ship-building, engineering and architecture. Many old churches along the West Coast have been designed and built by my ancestors. It could come as a surprise to many, if they knew that the famous floating dock in the UK was built in Mumbai and towed all the way to Portsmouth. It was in service in the dockyard until the early eighties for maintenance of submarines and small craft.

The land and property owned by my ancestors were the subjects of envy of people who came to Mumbai later from other parts of India to exploit the economical prosperity of the city. Why the later generations of some indigenous Mumbai people did not keep the control of these assets is now a part of history. Perhaps this might be attributed to their carelessness, trust in others and, perhaps, to their excessive tastes in wine and women.

The last straw came quite recently in the late eighties. The Indian Government decided to help lower caste people with greater zeal and more generous education grants, social welfare and housing benefits. This meant cuts in meeting the needs of other genuinely deserving people. Some bright politician decided that our community suffered unduly from the disadvantage of neither being in the uppermost layer of the caste system like Brahmins nor in the lower caste group among the scheduled classes. The solution was to reclassify the community as "carpenters", so that it became a part of the less developed group of communities. This must have hurt the feelings of the older generation, who knew about their origin and the warrior-like qualities of the ancestors. However, the life goes on and there could always be another turn of the wheel and revival of the good old days.

2
Early Days

*I*t was a dark evening in October 1940, in a small part of Mumbai. The air was warm and sultry, after a typical day in the Indian summer. The atmosphere in the house was stifling with grief. An old lady, my grandmother Nani, was very ill.

In those days in 1940, the medical help in Mumbai was not reliable. Apart from some commonly known general medicines available in shops, people relied on treatment given by knowledgeable elders. They usually had a cloth bag containing dried herbs, tree barks and roots, which could be ground and boiled to make a tea-like drink. A horn of an antelope (Samber-shing) would be rubbed against a smooth piece of stone to form a paste with little water, which was applied to the forehead to provide relief from cold and headache. Children invariably got a generous dose of castor oil as a purgative, since bad stomach was considered to be the root cause of their bad health.

Ladies were quite careless about their health and would sleep off an illness instead of taking any medicine, until it was too late. Falling ill was considered to be a blemish, arising from laziness or some sinful act. Old-fashioned ladies like Nani preferred to tough out any illness, until they became bedridden. Even then, they would not moan or complain. Married women often believed, in their old age, that death would be quite welcome as an invitation from the God ahead of their husbands. The best help was acceptable in the form of some Ayurvedic medicine called *matra*. This would just reduce the suffering, so that all immediate relatives, wives or husbands, sons and daughters could bear the painless passing away of a revered member of the family.

My uncle Hari was the main figure at Nani's bedside, being her eldest son. He was appropriately melancholy and had a couple of strong drinks to enable him to bear the grief. He was afraid of losing his widowed mother and the support she had provided to the family after his father's death. Some old ladies were by my grandmother's bedside, wiping her face and sobbing in unison at the same time. Their main role was to monitor her breathing and decide if she was still in this world. All was quiet until one of them screamed,

"It's all over!"

Hari gave a loud cry of anguish. He suddenly rushed out to the other room, where a frail young lady was nursing her baby. He snatched the little thing and shook it above his head. He then ran to the window and shouted,

"I am going to chuck you out of the window, you little runt! You killed my mother!"

The silence was broken and a pandemonium of various tones of groaning and moaning followed, expressing sorrow and fear at the same time. Hari stopped at the window momentarily. Maybe he was uncertain of what he should really do. He might have felt the effect of the shock or perhaps the country liquor had slowed him down a little after the quick dash to the window. Suddenly, as if by some divine intervention, one of the old women by Nani's bedside shouted so loud that she was heard in spite of the general upheaval,

"Oh God, You are merciful! She is alive!"

Hari's anger subsided as quickly as it had risen. He put the baby down and started weeping aloud himself. Someone took this chance to lift the baby and place it safely back in the mother's arms, who was too stupefied to react.

All this sounds pretty melodramatic but it happens to be my own ordeal soon after my birth. I was born for the second time! Although I survived that brief encounter with death, I was apparently shocked too badly. I kept still for some time, causing deep anxiety among a group of adults who had moved away from Nani and gathered around my mother. I was taken ill soon afterwards with typhoid and had high fever for some days.

At one time, my dear mother held me motionless in her arms. The old ladies came to keep a watch with the same intensity as they had done near Nani's bedside earlier. I was meant to die but it also did not happen under the gradual effect of fever, just as it had not happened under the quick-temper action of my uncle.

This little episode was to be the first drama in my life, narrated to me many times by my dear aunt, when I grew up. It seems, however, that the early shocks left their mark and I grew up as a weak child, with stunted growth and my body like a virtual skeleton during my teenage days. My mother remembers my two encounters with death and the way Nani loved and cared for me, after her own recovery from illness, until her very last days.

3
My grandfather's times

My mother's father, Nanaji, was one of the most intelligent persons among his contemporaries. He served with a construction firm under an Englishman, Mr Bailey by name. He was a favourite employee, a loyal and honest man with infallible skills with numbers and calligraphy. He led a good life, just like most of the well to-do gentlemen of his time. He was known to be partial to alcohol and so generous that he often paid for rounds of drinks without any hesitation. People from my community were known for such generosity and for losing their fortune in pursuit of wine

My grandfather

and women. One of my friends told me about a popular belief among the present generation of other communities,

"Do you know, Babu, why your ancestors lost their houses and ours didn't, although both drank and chased women? Your lot paid and ours just enjoyed!"

Nanaji used to go to work in a popular office area called "Fort", about three miles from his home. He would start from home late in the morning, as the custom used to be, after a meal combining breakfast and lunch. He had his own transport in the form of a one-horse cart (oddly known as a Victoria), hired on monthly terms. He usually gave lift to one or two of his relatives, who also worked near his office. If someone were to be delayed, others would wait in the corner public house or a *gutta*, and have a drink. The fellow travellers were no respecters of punctuality and, occasionally, one drink led to the other. A similar routine was observed in the evening in reverse, after a hard day at work. The pain of missing each other had to be endured with some alcoholic fortification and the goodbyes were never short and formal.

Those who came home straight after work like Nanaji, perhaps after a drink or two, were really the good guys. Some were not as good and chose to spend part of the evening elsewhere. Indians of older generation often claim that the moral standards were higher in India during the earlier part of the twentieth century than those in the sixties and the following decades. However, one should be forgiven for not fully believing in this, after listening to some anecdotes about people of Nanaji's times in Mumbai and in other parts of India. Probably, indiscretion of men and adventures of married men in higher circles were understood as "it is all right for some". They were often tolerated, unless anyone was made to suffer on their account. No one was really enthusiastic about bringing everything out in the open for the sake of it, which came later and grew into the ugly "Media" mentality. Many upper class families genuinely contributed to the society, helped the religious festivals and assisted those with temporary financial problems. It is conceivable, therefore, that some occasional and unfortunate slip-up on the part of a young person from such families was overlooked. People believed that the family would get over the bad patch in the end and keep up the good work of their forefathers. The overall well-being of the society and the sense of community were held in high regard and the equilibrium was kept inherently stable for many generations. This may have changed in the later part of the twentieth century, particularly after India gained independence. Mumbai began to attract people from all over India in search of work and money. In many respects, this was inevitable from the national point of view. However, the local community culture in Mumbai was lost for ever.

Along with the indiscretions of young men, I have also heard a few tales from one of my aunts about extra-marital relationships of smooth operators belonging to the so-called good families. Young widows and spinsters were vulnerable to the advances of such characters and clandestine relationships were known only to some and not talked about in public. An upper class gentleman admirer of a spinster or a married woman of a lower social status would assume a disguise of an uncle or a benefactor from her parental connections. It caused some embarrassment to the poorer family but not a permanent social stigma as such. All was forgotten eventually and the bigger picture remained as that of a stable and virtuous society.

My mother told me once about a young widow who was very fond of her brother Hari as a young boy of about twelve. The widow was also friendly with some older boys, which seemed quite sweet of her and natural to all the families at that time. One day the woman suddenly disappeared and her family told others that she had gone on a pilgrimage to a holy place called Nasik. It transpired later that such pilgrimage was meant for spending the period of pregnancy far away from the home town. Such holy cities would be crowded and quite impersonal. Our forlorn female had taken refuge in a safe house, which could be trusted for its discretion. In this way, the woman could deliver the baby, instead of undergoing an abortion, and she could come back to the normal life in due course. Babies born as a result of such unfortunate liaison would grow up in orphanages and a few were adopted by childless couples. In those days, abortion was not available openly as an option and birth control measures were still to come. Under such circumstances, some poor women, who could not possibly afford to remain pregnant, are known to have resorted to such inhuman measures as eating broken glass. They either died prematurely or were disabled for the rest of their lives.

My grandmother

Whatever happened outside the home, Nanaji worshipped his wife Nani. In those days, a gentleman depended on his mother or wife for the stability of the household and half-obeyed her. This was the general tradition during about the first half of the twentieth century, which meant that husbands and sons would obey the ladies of the house only when it suited them! The ladies were not given any money in cash as a rule. Everyone believed that the ladies did not want to handle money, any way, and very few housewives could read and write well enough to keep accounts. The grocery and clothes were all paid for quarterly in arrears. The ladies got ornaments as inheritance and they kept them as their own treasure in their personal possession. The male folk had no right on those items. A devoted wife was supposed to keep this treasure as an insurance, just in case of a tragedy, for example, husband's long term illness. Health insurance or any such safety net was not available at that time. The sets of ornaments usually included bangles (rigid bracelets), necklaces and anklets, with genuine diamonds and precious stones put together in twenty-two carat gold. Any lesser quality was relegated to the status of "brass" and not gold. Pearls were real and not "cultured" or artificially farmed. Ornaments in silver or gold-plating were sneered at and only gypsies would wear such things.

The ladies of Nani's generation were disadvantaged to a degree that could not even be contemplated by the young women of the present. They had their homes, husbands and children on the plus side and the in-laws to contend with. Some were lucky to have loving mothers-in-law but, in some cases, the relationship could become adversarial. This was a classic case of the old matriarch seeking to keep the young pretender down under her authority. Complaints by such unkind mothers-in-law to the men could be seldom fabricated and most men believed the older ladies. A young man would rarely dare to take his wife's side or even sympathise with her, for the fear that he would be branded as traitor to his mother. Sex was a private and secret matter and often a matter of the "flesh". Pleasures of the flesh represented yielding to temptations and they could lead to sinfulness. This was in contrast with the holy characteristics of the mind or soul, which were associated with godliness. The analogy led to an image of wife as an object of "temptation", leading the son away from his duties to his mother, a symbol of godliness, virtues and the ultimate purity of the soul.

Besides, some mother would feel that her son deserved to be married to a girl from a better family. Allegations and incidents during the marriage ceremony, true or false, would be remembered for a long time; "meanness" of the girl's father, inadequacies in the dowry and gifts, slippage in observing a certain procedure or a lapse in conducting a ritual, etc. The situation was much worse if the bride came from some other town or village. The city and country divide was phenomenal. Country girls in city families were taunted as yokels and city girls were accused as having corrupted manners. In any event, the popular adage prevailed,

"Cows and women would get on with each other, only if they were from the same village!"

This imbalance would persist until the patriarch or head of the family was alive. After that, in a few unfortunate cases, the worm would turn. A widowed mother-in-law could face a life of misery, having lost her lord protector. She would also lose her symbols of authority, the right to wear "kum-kum" on her forehead and a black-beaded necklace called "mangal sutra" (holy thread). The revenge of an oppressed daughter-in-law was sometimes ruthless. With the shift in power, the husband would change his allegiance and seek refuge under the influence of the new lady of the house. Some excessive examples of this change are known to have resulted in chopping off the hair of the crest-fallen widow, restricting her to one meal a day, etc.

Generally, ladies of Nani's generation were tolerant and aware of their weakness and their strength. They would not have any experience in dealing with the outside world, and, therefore, they were content to depend on the men. However, the strength of character of a housewife was unquestionable, in dealing with matters concerning the household and the children. The husband did well to know his limits and that he would not risk stretching the feminine tolerance too far.

During holidays and on some special occasions, Nanaji often went to listen to music, with his friends to start with and, later on, on his own. They used to visit one of the houses run by professional women with traditional skills in vocal and instrumental music. This was accepted as a reasonable pastime for a breadwinner, if he could afford such expensive treats. However, listening to music could sometimes lead to stopping for a drink afterwards and then on to further intimacies with the artist. These artists were known to be very selective about such liaisons. However, if a relationship did blossom, the artist would remain faithful to her man. A few were even known for supporting errant clients during their difficult times or, in some rare cases, during their old days, out of affection and gratitude for their generosity during their younger days.

Nanaji was progressively drawn into such situation. He started spending more time and money with a certain singer called Rupa. Nani came to know about Nanaji's indiscretion and tolerated it for some time. If anyone asked about his whereabouts, she would say that he had gone for some entertainment! However, it became so bad that, for a whole month, the groceries were not paid for and the family had to survive on only beans and rice. The final stage was reached when Rupa hired a room in the adjacent building and this was too much for our Nani. She confronted the woman in public, caught hold of her hair and slapped her in the face. She ordered her to leave the locality at once and not to see her husband again. Nani declared that she could no longer bear the humiliation and hardships of her children, and she would burn herself alive if Rupa did not comply with her demands. Nanaji was brought into line and no one saw Rupa again. The chapter was finally closed and the life was back to normal.

Generally, men of Nanaji's generation were totally dependent on their mothers in their earlier lives and on their wives during their married lives. The crises would come and go but the family and home provided support all the time. One could rely on one's home as the safe haven to return from the stormy weather elsewhere. Pen-pictures of famous men include scenes of comfort they derived from the company of loving and dutiful women. These women had a mission in life to provide home comfort to their sons and husbands. In the days without radio and television, a man would come home, have his supper, finish any reading or writing and retire in the company of his wife. The conversation was often one-sided. The man would talk and the wife would sit at his feet and listen, adding an odd remark or two to keep the conversation going. I recall such scenes from the biography of a famous judge, Justice Ranade, written affectionately by his wife Ramabai, a famous lady herself for her part as a pioneer in the education movement for women. However, she cared for Justice Ranade so much that he would fall asleep while Ramabai would rub a little milk on the underside of his feet with a bronze cup, which was meant to relieve the tension and promote restfulness.

Unfortunately, such excessive dependence on one's wife or mother often inhibited development of strength of character in some cases, which would be essential for anticipating and dealing with unexpected changes and shocks in life. This was the case with Nanaji, who felt well protected by his family at his home. His work-place provided him with another shelter, where he showed his total allegiance to his duties to his employer and to his subordinates who depended on him.

Nanaji took great pride in his work. He served Mr Bailey with unquestionable integrity and loyalty. Mr Bailey was one of those British gentlemen, who had succeeded in winning over Indians from educated middle class, through their fairness and their own hard work. Such mutually compatible combination was perhaps one of the most significant factors responsible for keeping the British Government and commerce going for such long time in India.

In November 1923, Mr Bailey had to leave for England, just before the monthly pay-day for the workers. He would normally withdraw the sum required for the wages and hand it over in an envelope to Nanaji. On this occasion, the workers were expecting a bonus for Diwali, a festival closely comparable with Christmas in the western world. Diwali is celebrated with the utmost enthusiasm by all Hindu families, with decorative lights, plenty of sweets and gifts for the family. It signifies the happiness of farmers after bringing in a successful harvest. The businessmen open new books, after

Mr Bailey

offering prayers to Laxmi, the Goddess of wealth. All this requires extra cash and a bonus at this time means a lot to a working man.

Mr Bailey was at a meeting with clients on a construction site all day, to tidy up everything before he boarded the steamer later in the evening. He could not hand over the envelope to Nanaji personally and left a note saying that it would be in the office safe instead. Next day, Nanaji went to work, found the note and opened the safe. Unfortunately, the envelope was not there! The poor man stood dumbfounded for a while. His assistants were waiting outside, wondering what sort of bonus was in prospect, since that year had been a good year for the firm. Nanaji somehow closed the safe and collapsed in his chair. The shock that the workers could not be paid was too much for him to bear, since it was his personal responsibility to pay them. The days of ship-to-shore telephone connections were still to arrive and Mr Bailey could be contacted only by a telegram. The news soon spread and the festive mood turned into a gloom. The workers were concerned for Nanaji's health and someone took him home safely. Somehow, Nanaji's assistant contacted one of Mr Bailey's financiers and convinced him about the seriousness of the situation. Fortunately, people did trust each other in those days and Mr Bailey's credit was good for the sum of money involved.

At Nanaji's home, gloom and darkness of the evening contrasted with the joy in other houses and lights on the street. Nani was distraught and, for once, could not see any way forward. She mustered enough strength to look after the youngsters. Unfortunately, Nanaji's illness proved to be more serious than just a shock. The middle-aged man did not have the mental strength required for bearing up with this eventuality. When he first woke up, he opened his eyes as if he was staring into some vacuum. Then he sat up and enquired aloud if the police had come. His old assistant was sitting by his side and reassured him that no one would ever dream of holding him responsible for the loss of money. He assured Nanaji that the staff would do a thorough search for the envelope and it would surely be found soon. But Nanaji was delirious and quite unable to understand anything the loyal assistant was saying. He carried on shaking and talking to himself,

"I know they will come for me soon. Oh God, I know you are putting me to the test."

This was probably the result of images he had in his subconscious of the old saints who were put to such stern tests by the God. It could also be the fear of the law and the cases he might have heard about the general inadequacy of the judicial system. The joint effect of his helplessness and the sense of responsibility for the workers had weakened him so much that his self-confidence was totally destroyed. His mind was incapable of any rational judgement and he remained bedridden, getting weaker and weaker every day.

At last, after some four weeks or so, a telegram arrived from Mr Bailey. It said that the envelope was stuck in his briefcase and travelled to England with him. He had apologised fervently and hoped that the money had been arranged for paying the workers. Nanaji's assistant was overjoyed and went straight from the office to see his unfortunate colleague. In his enthusiastic mood, he rushed to Nanaji's bedside and exclaimed,

"Look, Nanaji! the money has been found after all. We all knew that it was not your fault."

The poor messenger had no idea of the psychological blow he had delivered to the feeble mind of the patient. Nanaji barely opened his eyes, smiled and passed away without uttering a single word. He had rushed to his creator like a little boy would run to his father and could not stop on the way before telling his father that he had passed his examination!

4.
Uncle Hari

*U*ncle Hari was the only son of his parents. My aunt Seeta was the eldest, five years older than Hari and thirteen years older than my mother. As a child, Hari was bright and very methodical. He had learnt by heart all multiplication tables for numbers up to "twenty-nine tens are two hundred and ninety". He could recite similar one-to-hundred tables for fractions, from a quarter up to "three and a quarter". His English was exemplary by old standards, especially the grammar, learnt through memorising spelling and declination of irregular verbs. He had inherited

Uncle Hari

Nanaji's skills in calligraphy and his joined-up hand-writing was beautiful.

His childhood hobbies were not the same as other boys of his age. After school, he would go quietly to the small patio behind the house and arrange pieces of timber and small stones to make models, using strings to hold the timber together. He would dress with utmost care, bathe twice a day and pray for half an hour reciting Geeta in Sanskrit with flawless pronunciations. He would wear a mark of sandalwood paste on his forehead, a symbol of devotion, and he would look every inch a Brahmin boy. My mother often told us a story about his visit to a friend's house. When the lady of the house saw Hari at the entrance, she hid away the freshly purchased fish, as it was considered impolite to display the fish in the presence of a Brahmin!

The eldest sister Seeta was the most fortunate. She was married in a wealthy family at the age of fifteen, during the best times enjoyed by the household. Her husband was the only son and heir to three large houses in the town and one estate and rice field in a village near Mumbai. Nanaji spared no expenses and Seeta simply went from one bed of roses to another. She was pretty and her photograph with the full set of ornaments and a dark green sari, was very much like that of the goddess Laxmi herself.

The situation of the household became very difficult after Nanaji's death. Nani controlled her grief for the sake of children. The grocery bill had been recently settled. The house was their own and Nanaji's last salary was brought home by his assistant. For the next three months, the family could have coped with the cash and the food situation.

According to the common tradition, relatives came to visit, mostly well meaning but some with other motives. There was no shortage of free advice, which would not cost them anything. It included suggestions for selling away the jewellery and the house. The visitors were often tactless and, although most of them came with good intentions, the family felt much worse after their visits. Instinctively, Nani warded off all pressures and inducement for selling away her property and ornaments. She was wise, because they would have fetched much less than their real value in those circumstances.

My mother had to suffer a lot during this time, being a little girl and unable to understand the full implications of the situation. A few old women even referred to her as a potential liability for the unfortunate family in the future, since she was not pretty as her older sister Seeta. Nani had decided to let my mother study, which was frowned upon by some. Children's education was Nani's first priority, firmly fixed in her mind. She was determined to act carefully, in spite of the calamity and the panic-laden advice of relatives.

At the time of Nanaji's death, Seeta was eighteen and a month into her first pregnancy. She was informed of the tragedy in the most tactful manner by her in-laws. They were a shade more concerned about the state of health of the young *grihlaxmi* (goddess of the house) than the disaster befallen on Hari and the other children. However, Seeta came to see her mother in difficulties, as often as she could. My mother, who was just a five-year old child, would have fared far worse without her big sister's compassion and support. Seeta took her to her home occasionally, where the little girl could have some respite from the sadness shadowing her own home.

Within some three months of Nanaji's death, Mr Bailey returned from England. This was probably the quickest he could manage, allowing for the time taken by the sea-voyage in those days. One of the employees came to Nani's house to say that Mr Bailey would visit them the next day.

The atmosphere in the house before Mr Bailey's visit was extremely solemn and perhaps, very strange. During the first year of mourning, a widow would normally not meet anyone, let alone a sahib. Mr Bailey had sent a word that he did not wish to see anyone other than the family. This caused some resentment among a few neighbours and relatives. They would have liked to come and bow before the great sahib. They would also have showed him the way they cared for the unfortunate family. Mr Bailey had some idea that such scenes might take place. He was too much of an Englishman to tolerate such show and cause embarrassment to the family of his departed friend and colleague.

When Mr Bailey arrived, Nani sat just behind the door to listen to Hari's translation of Mr Bailey's words. He entered, took off his shoes and hat and sat on the carpet on the floor.

"Madam, I beg your forgiveness for my mistake, which is the cause of all this sadness."

He spoke slowly and with genuine feelings.

"Your loss is immensely greater than anyone else's. I have lost a friend too and the firm is deprived of a trusted associate. Now that I have come, I shall try my best to help and ensure that you would have nothing to worry about any more."

Hari narrated this to the family, when he was in an agreeable mood once, as effectively as he would have recited Geeta. He spoke with his eyes fixed on two large photographs, which were seen prominently side by side in his large sitting room, one of Nanaji and the other of Mr Bailey.

Nani was speechless during this meeting. Hari was doing his best with the translation, but there was no real need. Mr Bailey left quietly after one hour or so. The visit included only a few more words and most of the time was filled with a dignified silence. Before leaving, he asked Hari about the cash situation. The quarterly grocery bill was due to be paid and Mr Bailey knew it. He left an envelope on the table and said,

"Listen to me carefully, young man, you are the head of the family now! I am not giving you anything other than what really belonged to your father. Come and see me tomorrow in the office, with some of your school homework notebooks. We shall see what we can do."

Unknown to anyone, Mr Bailey emptied all the money in his pocket in front of the garlanded photograph of Nanaji. He had not come to give just something but he wanted to do everything he could, not as a charity but with his heart filled with a genuine sense of duty.

Hari went to see Mr Bailey the next day with samples of his hand-written work. He did not have to wait long. Mr Bailey took him in by his hand, as if he were his own nephew. Hari expressed a wish to train as a civil engineer, but he insisted on doing it on part-time basis. He wanted to work and support his family. The only place with such facility at that time was a school in Sukkhar in north India. (This town is now in Pakistan.)

Hari was about fifteen when he enrolled to study building and engineering as an external student, under an overseer's diploma course, as it was known at that time. My mother has often told us about the hard work he used to put in. He would wake up at five every morning and, after bath, recite Geeta aloud for half an hour. This must have given him strength for the rest of the day but no one, well or unwell, could sleep much longer after he had woken up. Nani had to wake up well ahead of him to get the warm water ready for him first and then his breakfast. This routine was not open to debate and it was accepted by everyone dutifully.

Hari must have had a very steep learning curve. Mr Bailey saw to it that he developed his love for discipline and precision to make him an engineer in the true British tradition. Hari developed a no-nonsense style of carrying out construction work, employing his grasp for understanding all details thoroughly and without ignoring anything. The other staff members realised that he was destined for higher things, well above his father's achievements. He was sincere and honest like his father but he was also ruthless, intolerant and ambitious.

Mr Bailey did not hesitate entrusting Hari with difficult tasks. He soon asked him to undertake some responsible work on his own. Within some ten years of joining the firm, Hari was working as the sole person in charge of small work-sites. At the age of thirty-five, he became a partner. He visited England and Australia to develop the firm's capability with new plant and machinery. Mr Bailey retired soon after India became independent and he went back to England in 1950 for good. Hari was one of the two senior partners, who took over the firm.

His pursuit of career left him no time for much else, let alone the follies of youth common among young men of his age. He had a drink sometimes but at parties away from home and out of sight as far as Nani was concerned. Arranged marriages were the order of the day. I believe that Nanaji had expressed a wish in the company of one of his relatives that he would like his son to marry a girl from certain family. It had to be so, and the marriage took place in 1933.

In my younger days, I had a feeling that uncle Hari deserved a little better. His wife was my "big auntie" as regards her status and she always treated me very well. But her looks were not quite what one would expect of the wife of a successful engineer. She was short and, therefore, seemed rather big. Her left eye was a little squint and she spoke with a village accent, mostly much louder than normal. Her education was very limited. All she knew was to cook well and look after her husband and her mother-in-law. This she did well and, as far as one could tell, Nani was quite happy with her running of the household.

My relationship with uncle Hari was cold but big auntie was a warm-hearted person. I somehow became one of her favourite nephews, as my mother used to say at times. However, I felt guilty that I couldn't be equally cordial with her and her family. I could never be a snob but I did not like her family, particularly her brothers. There were seven of them, equally short and difficult to distinguish from each other if you did not know them well. It seemed that they came to see their sister only when my uncle was away. I wondered if their visits were meant for getting little hand-outs from their sister. I never found out what they did for living! It was none of my business really, but the thought that my uncle should have such brothers-in-law bothered me in my youthful days.

Uncle Hari was apparently content with his lot. When big auntie was at her parents' place for a couple of days, he used to invite my mother to his house. He could not stand the thought of eating out or eating meals cooked by servants without any proper supervision. My mother respected her big brother the same way as she had respected their father. She came home at noon after working as a teacher all morning and took me with her to her brother's house. She would arrange for her brother's evening meal, instruct the cook and servants thoroughly and saw that everything was in proper order. She would then return home to cook for my father, leaving me behind.

I would seek refuge in my uncle's reading room after my mother's departure. I read books like *Anand Ramayana,* one of the most popular versions of the epic. I stayed the night until my mother returned the next day. At the cost of missing a day at school, I really must have benefited from these visits. I was able to read books much advanced for my age, including some simplified versions of novels by Charles Dickens. In this way, I kept well out of sight from my uncle most of the time and I believe that he tolerated me, to say the least.

My uncle would return home at about six every evening. I used to hear him come from my seat in the reading room but I never came out unless he called me. When he did, I had to hurry and greet him with *Namaskara*, with palms of the hands put together close to the chest, and retreat back to the reading room.

He always went to work wearing a light coloured suit, a hat and black leather shoes. This distinguished him from other Indians and some would even call him a "brown sahib", with sarcasm and mostly out of jealousy. He was a true professional, thoroughly trained by a British engineer, and that was how he presented himself outside his home.

Once he entered his home, he would wash himself and change into Indian clothes, a dhoti and shirt. This would transform him and he was then a different person. He would enquire if anything had happened during the day that he should know. This would be answered by a suitable family member present at that time or by a trusted old lady servant. He would then ask the person to get the meal ready.

It was customary for men and boys to eat first and the females later on. My uncle would call me when the meal was ready. The routine was strict. One washed hands and feet and sat on a raised board placed behind a plate containing the first instalment of food. Legs would be folded and the ankles tucked in tightly in the form of a position described in the Yoga. Then I had to wait until my uncle said a brief prayer and sprinkled little water around his plate. This was a Hindu version of saying grace. Meal was taken in silence and the food was picked up with fingers, rice and vegetables or fish curry on Wednesdays and Fridays. The fingers should never be coated with food beyond the second joint and the thumb had to be used to promote the food in the mouth, without spilling anything. Slurping noises and burps were prohibited. One would eat not too slowly and not too fast. I used to glance at my uncle's plate through the corner of my eye and adjust my speed accordingly. The best thing I learnt from him was to clean the plate and I would never waste even a grain of rice.

After the meal, my uncle would sit down and ask me a question or two. Deep down in his mind, he felt for me a little and, perhaps, he remembered my illness as a baby. When a few minutes passed and no further question came my way, I did my *Namaskara* again and went back to the reading room.

Mostly, big auntie returned before my mother came to collect me late in the afternoon. We would leave at about half past six or seven, after my uncle returned from work, and go home for our evening meal. For some reason, this period of about less than one hour was the worst for me. I would virtually brace myself and hope to go home as soon as possible. Almost every time, within a few minutes of settling down, my uncle would call me. Knowing that his wife was back in the house, he would ask me aloud,

"Hey, how much is twenty-seven times seven?"

This would vary from "two and three quarters times fifty-seven", etc. I hated this and, some times, gave a wrong answer. My mother believed that one should learn by heart tables only up to twenty and no more. She did not believe in cramming up and memorising numbers like parrots. On the contrary, she encouraged me to work out some basic problems for myself. For example, many of my school friends would not bother to know why $(-3)\times(+2)$ should be (-6) and $(-3)\times(-2)$ should be $(+6)$. Even now, many people are content to press the buttons of the calculator and get the answer. The simplest way to understand this is to give meaning to the signs, plus meaning forward or credit or better-off and minus meaning backward or debit or worse-off. Then the multiplication of numbers with signs becomes a question, for example, asking for the effect of giving away £3.00 every day after two days in the future. Here, the sum of £3.00 has a negative sign and the period of two days in future has a plus sign. The answer (-6) means that I shall be £6.00 worse-off in two days time. Similarly, with the rate of giving away three pounds per day (-3), I should have been £6.00 better-off $(+6)$ two days ago (-2).

However, my uncle expected me to just memorise the multiplication tables and he had no time for the basics. If my answer was not correct, he would smile as a mocking gesture, which would hurt me a little.

I never really understood why he did this, but, after two or three occasions, I grew immune to it! Perhaps he had a dual or multiple personality. His mind might have had distinctly separate compartments. At work, he was a British civil engineer. But he had none of the other western characteristics or influence of any western ideas like child psychology on his mind. He believed in the old Indian way of life and reading Geeta gave him his mental strength. He believed in omens, someone's company or birth casting bad spell on someone else, etc. This did not somehow conflict with his engineering or his brush with the sciences. He probably thought of science only as a tool. Remembering tables and prescribed rules by heart was all he wanted from it and it would not influence him to question anything else in life.

My uncle did not single me out for such treatment and he was nasty to many other youngsters as well. Perhaps he meant to show that he was no soft touch with the youngsters. Probably, he might have used such method for arousing strong feelings in the young minds. He might even have risked being unpopular, by dispensing with the routine of showing good-mannered kindness and love to all youngsters. If this was the truth, he succeeded in my case, since I made up my mind to be a civil engineer. Perhaps my uncle's behaviour helped me to work hard and to keep me motivated to try my best to surpass him.

Big Auntie did not like the treatment my uncle handed out to me. Occasionally, she circled her finger over her head to reassure me and to indicate that her husband was little eccentric. I knew a few other grown up people in those days, with some similarly peculiar mannerism. However, I found it much easier to deal with them with tactfulness than to react, so that they were discouraged from carrying on with their odd ways.

Uncle Hari was somewhat less fortunate regarding his children. Only two of his children survived, his daughter Devayani followed by his son, Deepu. My mother told me that, before Devayani's birth, big auntie had lost two sons, who had lived only for a month or two. When Deepu was born, a priest advised Hari not to dress him with brand new clothes. Deepu had to wear clothes used by other babies first and then given to him, until he was three years old. Youngsters like me were told that this was the trick to hide him from the Lord of Death. The theological meaning was much deeper, as it was explained to me later on, although I did not understand it well. A cousin or son of a friend of the family, nearly of the same age as Deepu, would come to Hari's house, dressed with new clothes. The little boy's parents would undress him and put some other clothes on him. The priest would first bless the clothes worn earlier by the boy and then Deepu would wear them. I never questioned whether there was any real point in this ritual, as this did not make much sense. However, this practice did Deepu no harm and he grew up normally, which was the most important point.

Hari's western frame of mind would show up at home in some instances. His children had English nicknames. Deepu was called Jimmy and Devayani became Mississippi or Mishi for short. This was quite contrary to his traditional home image. My uncle addressed his children with nicknames, although he did not mind if others used their proper Indian names!

For me, Deepu was always Deepu, but the girl's name somehow stuck in my memory as Mishi. Perhaps Mishi sounded like an Indian word. It actually means "moustache" in Marathi. Some women might have a hint of hair over their upper lips but Mishi grew up to be without anything of the sort! She was a little on the heavier side, dark in complexion and rather shy and less sociable. This might have been made worse by her love for food, which made her even slower and less sociable as a child. Unfortunately, it did not help her when she became the butt of her father's jokes from time to time. Whenever he wanted some writing to be bigger and bolder, for example, he would ask it to be made to look like Mishi!

In 1955, my uncle moved from his smaller house to a bigger place in the suburb. Deepu took to the new environment quite well. However, Mishi did not do well at school there. She left school and did some training as a nurse for a while. Later on, she got into some bad company in the neighbourhood. I understand that she ran away with some lower class fellow. It was alleged that he had an eye on my uncle's money. Uncle Hari was very sad and sold that house immediately and moved elsewhere. I was away from home, studying at the engineering college in Ahmedabad at that time, and I did not quite get to know the whole story. I often wondered whether it was just a misfortune that could have happened to anyone or whether it was the result of Mishi's development as a child.

In 1968, I left Mumbai for England. I almost lost touch with uncle Hari, apart from some mention about him in my mother's letters now and again. He was out of Mumbai during my visit in 1974 and I couldn't see him. Deepu was married and the family seemed quite well at that time.

In November 1979, during Diwali time, I came to Mumbai on holiday with my wife and daughter. We rented a flat in the suburbs, as there was not enough space in our house in Dadar. This happened to be within walking distance of where my uncle and Deepu lived. My uncle knew that we were in the neighbourhood. Remembering my childhood days, I decided to wait for my uncle to invite us. We were soon invited to spend an evening with them.

Deepu had done very well in his career by that time. He worked in a subsidiary of his father's firm. Uncle Hari had really retired and he would only be called up to visit a site occasionally, to sort out some problems. Big auntie was very happy with Deepu, her daughter-in-law and her grandson. Everything seemed to have turned out very well in the end for my uncle!

We went to see uncle Hari, all suitably dressed and at the appointed time. I took a bottle of good Scotch malt whiskey with me, knowing that my uncle would like it very much. He seemed to be very happy to see us and invited my daughter to sit on his lap. I handed over the bottle to him discretely, so that big auntie would not notice it. My wife and I sat down but Deepu was still standing. My wife moved over a little, but he would not sit down.

"Jimmy does not sit down in my presence!"

Hari said quietly, so that my wife could just about hear him. Same old man, I mused in silence! I was fortunate that my wife had the good sense to refrain from asking for the reason. It was meant to be a mark of respect, I explained to her later, although I was unsure whether she would find it logical or otherwise!

Big auntie was truly delighted to see us, perhaps more than her husband. She wanted to talk and did so when she asked me to come into the kitchen under some pretext. Her simple and uncomplicated nature showed through her questions and my eyes moistened a little.

Deepu asked my wife her preference for drinks, for her and for the girl. Some orange juice seemed all right, since the meal was to be served after a few hours, when we would come back from a little run-around in Deepu's jeep. I could read the anxiety on my wife's face since no one had asked me. Again, to her eternal credit, she kept quiet!

The refreshment came on a silver plate. For me, there was a silver bowl with warm and sweetened milk, lashed with sliced almonds, pistachios and saffron. I told my wife later that big auntie always gave me the same drink, when I visited her on some auspicious days like Diwali. This was something to do with a tradition to honour the eldest son of the husband's sister. I could not explain why but I was accustomed to the ways big auntie would treat me. I had never asked her for any logical explanation for anything when I was younger and there could be no real reason to do so when I had grown older!

After dinner, my uncle and I had a little chat. He seemed in good health and enjoying his grandchild. He had heard about my studies, my becoming a chartered engineer and publishing some papers in the UK journals.

"You have done quite well, haven't you Babu?"

He said so with some enthusiasm. His partner's son, Mr Deshpande, had made six attempts to pass the qualifying examination for gaining the chartered status and given it up. Mr Deshpande Senior used to describe how hard these examinations were. My uncle had let it slip that his nephew had passed it at the first attempt.

At last, I had made my peace with my uncle. It was worth waiting for so many years!

My uncle died in 1984. For me, he was a living record of a remarkable and successful union between the East and the West. Being a son of an old-fashioned Hindu Indian Nanaji did not place any barriers in his development as a British engineer, albeit owing to his good fortune of having Mr Bailey to help him at the right time in his life.

5
My Father

My parents were married when my mother was seventeen, some twelve years after Nanaji died. Those days were hectic. Hari was too occupied with his career-building and training. My mother had modest looks and the dowry was limited. An intermediary brought the information about a young man of about twenty-five years of age, handsome, with a job and without any brothers and sisters. Nani's relatives put pressure on her to clear her daughter's case and Hari had literally no time and little experience in such matters as arranging his sister's marriage.

The intermediary had said nothing about my father's life and his family. The investigation was limited and Nani had no other reliable source to check things out. Nani knew that the young man was the only son, looking after his widowed father, and nothing else. The proposal did not seem too bad to reject.

However, I must say that this episode exposed some basic deficiencies in the arranged marriage system of that time, in the thirties or forties. The bridegroom's side would be unfairly dominant and they would invariably dictate the terms. If the bride's side were to be as disadvantaged as that of Nani's family, the intermediaries would be anxious to pressurise them and look for a quick solution. Their role in the arranged marriage system was voluntary and a service to the community, which probably gave them a position of importance and prestige.

After so many years, any apportionment of blame must seem pointless. Whenever I tried to make enquiries out of curiosity, I could not get anywhere. My father had strictly forbidden us to talk about his past or ask anyone about it. I felt that some of the elders might have known about my father's background but they decided to be tactfully evasive. Before my father's death in 1996, none of my brothers or my sister would venture to talk about his life as a single man. We knew that our father's childhood had been difficult and someone would even make an occasional unkind comment about his past. However, we got used to ignoring such things and got on with our lives.

The best information I could get about my grandfather was that he lost his wife when my father was little over a month old. My grandfather used to drink very heavily and he had other vices as well, including women and gambling. As the story went, he had followed his father's footsteps and even surpassed him in many respects. Between these two, they managed to squander all the wealth and lost two houses and all the family fortune to their debtors. The ladies were forced to lead lives full of misery. The only consolation, if it could be so described, was that both my grandfather and my father had no brothers and sisters.

My grandmother suffered from problems during her pregnancy and childbirth and she never recovered. Children were born at home in those days, with only an experienced old lady present as a midwife. The proportion of infant deaths and deaths of young mothers was high. The situation was really hopeless for an expectant mother, if she were to be weak on account of some illness. My grandmother suffered from this ordeal, which had its inevitable sad ending.

Worse was to come in my father's life one morning just before the Hindu New Year day in April 1910. My grandfather took his three month old son to his neighbour's house, a priest in a famous temple in Mumbai. He begged his neighbour to keep the baby in his care. The bailiffs were closing in on him and he wanted to abscond, since he could not bear the thought of going to jail. He confessed to the neighbour that his relatives and people of his own community would not even open their doors to him. He would have killed himself and his son, but he did not have the courage to do so.

I was told by one of the priest's relatives that he was a god-fearing and honest man, who had a son and a daughter of his own. The poor old priest could not have expected to hear this extra-ordinary confession of his errant neighbour. He must have paused a little, but his wife rushed forward, quite unlike any other ladies of her time, and virtually snatched the baby from its miserable father. My grandfather walked away and no one saw him for the next twenty-four years.

He spent the time wandering from place to place and ended up in Benares, a holy place on the banks of the river Ganga. Finally, he was taken ill and, perhaps, he would have died like any other vagrant. However, a kindly pilgrim took pity on him and brought him to Mumbai to the priest's house, where my father also lived at that time.

My father went to school and studied until he was fourteen. He was a bright student but his benefactor had no real interest in education. Most boys studied up to the age of fourteen and then the family decided whether a boy should go for matriculation. This was a fairly prestigious examination, equivalent to the secondary school certificate of the present. However, the standard of this qualification was far higher in those days, as could be said about education at all levels generally. One could get a very good white-collared job with this qualification and, therefore, it was very desirable indeed. My father could have achieved this but his sense of gratitude prevailed on him. He could not burden the family any longer than necessary and took up employment in a textile mill as a trainee. He paid the family a sum of money every month from the day he got his first wages, as if he belonged to them. He continued to do so while his benefactor was alive. He would have carried on as the priest's son and perhaps got married with someone from their community. However, the return of his father changed his life and he had to move to a small apartment with his invalid father.

My mother had a torrid time in the early days of marriage as a seventeen year old exposed to the strange circumstances. My father really had no idea about the need for tenderness towards a young girl. His father, although an invalid, turned out to be quite a villain. He used to make my mother's life difficult by fabricating stories about her neglecting him. The poor girl was distressed and had nowhere to turn. She would not go to her mother to add to her own difficulties. After twelve months of causing miseries to my mother, my grandfather died. One should not say unkind words about a dead person, but it was indeed a good riddance.

After my grandfather's death, my mother decided to work as a teacher. Nani knew her problem and suggested that a career would be the best solution, Besides, my father's salary was not so large that she could save money for the time when children would come along. Nani was right in letting her study as a girl and her education was enough for her to start as a primary school teacher. My mother must have found the dual role difficult, as a teacher and a mother, when my sister was born. By the time I was born in 1940, an old aunt had come to live with us, which provided some relief for my mother.

When uncle Hari had the true knowledge about his sister's lot, he became very sympathetic towards her in his own way and my father became a villain in his eyes. This somehow meant that I, as my father's son, would be bad like my father. My sister, a female offspring and who resembled Nani a little, was on the good side or his side. The readers may see his frame of mind more clearly, leading to his outburst at the time of Nani's illness, soon after I was born.

In spite of all this, Hari and my father had a few things in common. For example, both of them liked precision. They strove to do well what was expected of them. By nature, both of them were rather indifferent towards society and relatives. However, Hari had some tolerance and tactfulness, necessary for socialising when it was essential to do so as the head of a family. He got these attributes naturally as a member of a stable family. My father lacked in both. He knew that he had to work to support his family. He also knew that he was good in his job. He cared very little for anything else. He never attended any functions or dinners at weddings. Whenever we were invited, one of the children would go with our mother. If the ceremony was over two days, as most weddings would be in those days, my mother would return home to cook for my father. I understand that he had been the subject of derision once or twice in early days. Someone made a comment about his father, there was an argument and that was the last time he attended a celebration dinner or a wedding party.

My father was an atheist and free thinker. He would, however, bow in front of a shrine. This was more out of politeness than devotion. He did not believe in practising religion and rituals, with only one exception. He would go to the funerals of the departed friends and relatives, although he would not attend the functions meant to mark the thirteenth day or the first anniversary.

In fact, he would be expected to attend when a tragedy occurred in the neighbourhood. If there was a knock on the door in the middle of the night for such a reason, he would go. Hindu cremations were not carried out by "Funeral Directors" in those days. Besides, the funeral had to take place within ten to twelve hours if the death took place at the person's residence or from the time the body was released by the hospital. Friends and relatives would manage the task as a duty and responsibility as members of the community and society. My father was one of the few people who knew the procedure. With the limitation on time being an important factor, one had to know how to arrange the municipal certificate, procurement of the material for the stretcher to carry the dead body to the place of cremation, etc. I never found out how he came to know all this. With his natural aptitude towards precision and methodical working, people believed that there could be no problems when he was with them. Later in the seventies, people got used to the idea of cremation in a municipal crematorium. Services of funeral directors became available and the custom of carrying the body of the departed on shoulders of near relatives was replaced by carriages.

Compared with my father, the most significant points in Hari's favour were the strength given by his religious upbringing and his good fortune to have met Mr Bailey at the right time in his life. My father had only the devotion to his work on his side. He was hard-working, honest and loyal to his employer. The life in a textile mill was not easy and hard work did not always get rewarded. He must have had some frustrations. I should know because we suffered with him when he did. He would be very bad tempered and my mother would be very unhappy. However, he would soon try harder and did quite well in the end to get a head-jobber's position.

During the period just after Indian independence, a mass of refugees and people from north India came to Mumbai in search of work. My father was the head-jobber in the Carding Department in a big textile mill. His colleagues and even the lower-ranked supervisors could get a couple of hundred Rupees for providing work to a labourer. Many of the supervisors prospered and bought large houses. My father would have nothing of the sort. Some labourers under him got work fairly and they would bring sweets at Diwali. This was the most he would accept.

The worst thing for us was when we started school. I was rather small and lonely. Like most children. I could not tell my father anything about my school or studies since he simply could not be bothered. That was my mother's field and not his! However, I had some good fortune to start with. My mother's friend was my class teacher and she sheltered me from the bully boys. I would not go and play during the recess and did my homework instead. The headmaster once saw me and said that I was too good to be in that class and promoted me. This happened twice and I got the taste for success. I was not diffident any more since I had an advantage over the other boys, as they accepted me as a clever fellow. I owe all my early success as a child to this kind lady. She remained a good friend of my mother and her help was invaluable on many occasions, especially when I went to the engineering college away from home. She used to loan money without any hesitation, which made the funding for my stay in the college hostel a lot easier.

I would have loved to tell my father about my exploits at the school and at college. It must sound strange but he was content to know that I studied something to do with science subjects and that was all he wished to know.

I always tried to make contact with him and succeeded on some rare occasions. At the beginning of each school year, he would wrap my books with brown paper. He did this work superbly. He often brought home some things from scrap dealers, for example, a gramophone or an old clock. He would then dismantle them and build some other things using the spare parts. Once he made a fan, using the spring from a gramophone, which would circulate air as long as the spring could turn the wheel. It made some noise and the spring had to be rewound after every two hours. I helped my father to do this, which gave me the first experience with spanners, saws and screwdrivers.

Occasionally we used to talk but only when he wished to do so. The best I remember about him is the conversation we had in 1957, when I was at the University. He told me about his visit to a textile mill in Dhaka in 1938, for installing some imported machinery. (Dhaka is now the capital of Bangladesh.) This mill belonged to the owner of the mill where my father worked. The plant was imported from Germany and the manager of the textile mill wanted to have it commissioned forthwith. Unfortunately, the instructions were in German and no one understood the language. My father took the drawings and put the pieces together, mostly by using his imagination and logic. The plant was tested and commissioned.

Within a few days, the representatives of the German firm arrived and said, with the help of their own interpreters, that they had come to install the machinery. On hearing that it was already installed and running, they became aggressive and demanded an explanation for installing it without using their services. They showed the papers with a warning that the plant must be installed by experts only. The interpreter somehow clarified that the instruction was not followed because no one could read and understand German! This could have amused anyone else but it did not appeal the German sense of humour.

The burly leader of the delegation rushed to the plant and started examining it in a true Germanic fashion. The owner of the mill and his staff watched his frustration with mild amusement, as he could not find anything wrong with it! He calmed down and demanded to see the man who did it, first thing next morning. My father went to see him and the German treated him with the utmost courtesy. They offered him a job, including tuition in German and training in Germany for three years.

"Why didn't you accept?"

I exclaimed in amazement. I could see the advantage he would have had and the change in his life, and ours, which could have ensued.

"Your sister was little and your mother would have been on her own. How could I go, leaving my home and family here? Besides, I did not like the Germans and could not have worked for them. Haven't you read what they did in the war?"

He was probably right, in his own way. What he said to me would have made an Englishman proud. This episode just about summed up my father's outlook towards life!

He retired in 1975 at the age of sixty-five. He had become much more approachable by then. A few years later, my brother got married and his wife had a daughter. My father was very happy. He would look after the little girl with great affection. He would take her in his arms and go for a walk, forgetting all his worries.

He had retained his punctuality even in his retirement. He would wake up at about seven o'clock every morning. After bath he would have a cup of tea and light breakfast. He would read the newspaper and then look after his granddaughter. He would eat at 11.00 am and sleep under a tree in the garden on his armchair until 3.00 pm. Then someone, mostly my unmarried sister, would give him his tea. He would wake up and be with the little girl again. He had his evening meal at 8.00 pm and he would go to sleep at about 10.00 pm every day.

He had two rules that never changed. First, no one should wake him up, as he woke up by himself at the right time. Second, he would pick up his plate after a meal, or his cup after his tea, and take it to the kitchen sink and put some water on it. This way the plate or the cup would not dry up. He never did washing up but never let anyone else to clear his plate or his tea cup.

By 1990, both my brothers moved away from home. One went to the Middle East and the other had his own flat in the suburb. This made my father quite unhappy. However, there were other children in the neighbourhood around him for a little while. He had become rather weak by that time and, eventually, tended to be on his own more and more. Although he began to have some speech impediment, he could walk and keep himself clean without assistance, almost until the end.

On 26 June 1996, he had his meal and went to sleep in the garden as usual. My sister took his tea to him at 3.00 pm. When the cup was not returned to the kitchen until 3.45 pm, she got worried and went back to see him. He had left this world quietly, in his sleep on his armchair under a tree in the garden. My sister came back indoors weeping and a boy in the neighbourhood saw her. He came and helped my sister to bring my father indoors.

Word went around and within two hours, there were some hundred people gathered in front of the house. Some had just tears in their eyes for this lonely man. All of them stayed until 9.00 pm, when my brother had made arrangements for the funeral. By that time, there were some two hundred people in front of our house.

My father's will had clear instructions that he should be taken to the municipal crematorium for cremation on a carriage, and not on a stretcher on shoulders of any relatives. He did not want the traditional funeral on a spire by the seaside place meant for such purpose. Perhaps he did not trust others to make the funeral arrangements as properly as he would have done!

At the crematorium, there were no priests to recite any religious hymns and there were no traditional rituals. The man did not believe in rituals and wouldn't allow them even for his own last rites!

6
Dadaji

I met Dadaji in 1952 for the first time. He came to our house for collecting subscription for our community club. He was chairman of the Membership Committee and played a large part in introducing grants for education for poor children, aid for widows, etc. He had devised a system for payment of life-membership by instalments and this was most beneficial in boosting the membership and for raising funds for the club.

Dadaji

He was one of the most elegantly dressed gentlemen, who looked smart even in his late fifties. He wore a round black cap, a long coat and a white dhoti. Wearing dhoti is an art, which is almost extinct nowadays. It required some skill to keep the one-piece cloth, some eight metres long, at the right level round the waist without using any belt. The length had to be adjusted so that the dhoti covered the ankles and it did not slip down due to any body movements. Dadaji was one of the experts. He carried a stick with gold-plated grip and the end cap. Collecting subscriptions was considered to be a valuable service to the club. Unlike the modern times, people like Dadaji were received warmly as welcome visitors and everyone paid their dues promptly and without hesitation.

Dadaji knew about my progress at school and my father's nature. He also knew that I did not come in contact with many relatives and other community people on account of my father's way of life. Without making it obvious that he was doing me a favour, he asked my mother if I could accompany him on his trips for such community work. He said that he was getting rather old and I could be a great help. My mother was very happy and I started accompanying Dadaji about once a month on these missions. This was to be an invaluable experience for me and I did help Dadaji a little this way. We used public transport all the time and carried papers with us, which was a little easier for Dadaji with an assistant like me.

We went to various households, large and small and rich and poor. Dadaji's manners were the same everywhere, pleasant and courteous. He was a religious man but his views were wonderfully egalitarian. He would never underestimate or patronise anyone. His motto was to treat all people alike; the king and the road-sweeper, man and woman, an adult and a child. Of the three classes, treating adult and a child alike was rather unusual in those days. An adult would often rebuke a child for asking an awkward question with a tap on its head. The stock phrase was,

"Shut up, you imbecile! Don't try to be too clever!"

Mostly, this was said because the adult was too proud to admit that he or she did not know the answer. Dadaji never did this to me. He encouraged me to ask questions and either answered my question fully or undertook to find the answer if he didn't know it straight away. He practised what he preached!

Even with a child of three or four years age, he spoke in the same manner as he would talk to adults, instead of indulging in baby-talk. He insisted that the love and respect for one's mother-tongue had to be nurtured right from the beginning. It would be impossible to master other languages if we spoke our own language with indifference. It made sense to me when I had to write text in English about technical matters, instead of using drawings and formulae. The translation of thoughts into fluent written work or speech is an activity of mind. One should develop it first in the most convenient medium, which must be the mother-tongue. One should then look after this gift, keep it flowing and develop it to suit the use of other languages. However, one cannot learn other languages effectively unless the ability of converting thoughts in expression has its strong roots in the early stages, through one's mother-tongue.

Dadaji was well versed in Sanskrit and he prayed regularly, although not as long a duration as my uncle Hari did. Besides, Dadaji believed in the practical application of principles in scriptures like *Geeta,* more than indulging in the scholarly philosophy. He often quoted that the most important direction given in *Geeta* could be summarised as encouragement to say "Yes". Most problems in the Indian history seemed to originate from the tendency to disagree on trivial matters. On the other hand, if each party looked for merits in the other's point of view, they could find a convergent solution more easily. In situations where a party could not agree with the other, they should go their own ways and remain disinterested in what is not their preference, rather than fight to get their own way. I often wondered how valuable this advice would have been in resolving a number of international conflicts.

Dadaji was a strict vegetarian. He never drank tea or coffee and observed the days of fasting religiously, on Mondays and Thursdays. On these days, he would not eat anything other than one meal made with tapioca rice. Most people knew this and gave him either warm milk or lemon juice, when he visited them on these days. He was careful to avoid any offence or cause difficulties to the housewife. He would carry a few fresh limes in his bag and ask the lady of the house to prepare a glass of juice, if she could not offer him anything suitable. This was most useful when he visited a new home for the first time.

Dadaji had worked as a manager of a firm of timber merchants. He was comfortably off with a house of his own and a good pension, quite sufficient for him and his wife. He was an expert in judging various species of timber. He had visited far away places in Assam in north India, where his firm would buy the produce of certain areas of the forest in advance. Such advance deals would make good profit for the firm when the timber was cut down and marketed.

His other interests were poetry and music. He was among the rare connoisseurs of classical music, who would be specially invited to some concerts. The old-fashioned artists often insisted that the front row should be occupied by people who understood the music, rather than those who could just afford to be there.

He appreciated Indian poetry, both Marathi and Urdu. Urdu poetry goes back to the days of the Mughals. It must have been a rare coincidence that a Hindu had acquired a taste for Urdu poetry. Dadaji belonged to a small club, which had many Muslim members who treated him as a fellow enthusiast in this field.

For such a fine person as Dadaji, it seemed odd that he should be without any son, daughter or a grandchild of his own. His wife, Vahini as we called her, was a wonderful lady, cheerful and pretty even at the age of fifty something. Their young and unmarried son had died in the Second World War in Africa. It seemed that they had come to terms with the life that came their way. Dadaji was occupied with his social work and Vahini was committed to looking after him.

She was indeed a perfect match for Dadaji. I have always seen her, even early in the morning, clad perfectly and with elegance in a nine yard sari, her hair immaculately groomed, a red dot of kum-kum on her forehead and a welcoming smile on her face for visitors like me. She had a charming

Vahini

manner of thanking me for accompanying her husband on his trips, without making me feel uneasy. I went to their place only occasionally, mostly in the mornings, but it always turned out to be a good day for me whenever I saw her. By nature, she had the tendency to care for others as a mother would do.

One Saturday morning, Dadaji came to our house. It was not a prearranged visit or scheduled day for our outing. For such trips, I would mostly go to his house, which was nearer the railway station than ours. However, he came and asked me if I could go with him and spend a couple of hours. I was able to do so and my mother did not mind it either. I did not ask about our destination, just as I had never asked him such questions on any earlier occasion.

We walked for about twenty minutes and arrived at the "Home for Blind People". I had never been inside and I was amazed to see the occupants in a different light. It literally opened my eyes, when I saw a group of blind men and women at ease in their own world! Who says that a blind human being should spend a life of misery, blaming one's misfortune and moaning all the time? On the contrary, the young men and women in that place were humming music, practising crafts like basket-weaving and seemed happy working in groups. Behind these walls, they had their own world, where they were in control. The outside world did not seem to matter, where people expected them to be compliant, sorry for themselves and conscious of their blindness.

"Did you see my children, Babu?"

Dadaji said quietly, with a hint of moistened eyes behind his spectacles.

In a hall at the centre of the building, two groups of about eight or ten people were sitting, as if expecting someone. As soon as they sensed that we were approaching, one of them asked,

"Is that you, Dadaji? But who has come with you? We have got a message that Joshi cannot come today."

Dadaji exchanged a word or two and turned to me.

"Babu, you can read aloud very clearly, can't you?. Could you please read the notation for this lot for an hour or so?"

Unlike the graphical signs used for writing the western music score, combining the notes and the rhythm, Indian classical music lessons are written using letters, *sa, re ga, ma,* etc. The rhythm is separate and not an integral part of the score. I knew a little about the music and agreed to help out. After about an hour, the listeners seemed to be satisfied. Their understanding and memory were amazing and it was a pleasure to spend some time with them. Finally, a young girl got up and asked,

"I don't suppose you could spare us some time next Saturday, Babubhai?"

Her addressing me as *Bhai* or brother sent a sensation of delight through my body. In the past, so many women had easily succeeded in making me do something for them. I could never say no, once I was captivated by the power of persuasion in their eyes. Here, the little lady had no such power. All she had was a vibrant and musical voice, emerging from her half-parted lips. Her question was put with an assumption of a probable refusal and it touched my heart. My head lost and the heart won!

It seemed that Mr Joshi, who had the Saturday appointment for the past six months, was unable to oblige the youngsters any longer. I took his place and carried on for the next three years until I left Mumbai for my engineering studies. I could never forget the shear enthusiasm of my listeners and the uplifting atmosphere in the place. I hope that my good work is entered properly in the books of the heavenly gate-keeper, either St. Peter or his Hindu equivalent, *Chitragupta.* However, if he has missed it out like some wily accountants do from time to time, I am more than content with the time I spent in that paradise on earth!

After finishing my pre-engineering qualification course in Mumbai, I went away for studying civil engineering. Thereafter, I started training and work, which kept me very busy. I kept in touch with Dadaji and met him whenever I could. However, I lost my job when the Government cut down construction work by 50% after the conflict with China. In 1968, I left Mumbai and went to the UK. I almost lost contact with Dadaji, other than an occasional letter or exchange of a parcel through a friend. I met him for the last time when I went back to Mumbai on leave in 1974. Vahini had passed away in 1973 and Dadaji had moved in with his nephew in a flat in Malad, a suburb of Mumbai.

I found out the address and location of the place and arranged to see him one day, through someone I knew in that area. A young lady, wife of Dadaji's nephew, opened the door. At Dadaji's place, Vahini used to welcome visitors with a smile like a goddess. Those days were gone! Here, a modern Marathi young lady dressed in a full length gown instead of a sari, just let me in.

Our Dadaji was standing at the door of an internal room. I did not wait for anything else but rushed to him past the bewildered young lady. He had lost his health. I would not have believed that the loss of a life-partner can have such devastating effect on a person. But Vahini was not just his life-partner but a part of his life!

"Hey Babu, come and sit down!"

Dadaji spoke to me, summoning all his strength.

"You are a married man now, Yes? Why didn't you send me an invitation? I would have come to England for your big day!"

I felt a bit guilty but I was also pleased to see the sense of humour alive and well in his weakened body. After a few other exchanges, he opened his heart to me.

"Babu, you didn't think that I would have been unhappy to hear about your marriage to a foreigner, did you? My boy, I know you too well to believe that you would change and do anything wrong! Honestly, she has looked after you very well, hasn't she?"

This was not the time to answer but to listen.

"Babu, I know that you will never forget your origin and culture. Just like the religion, our music, prayers and literature are part of the soul. Soul is not hurt by weapons or burnt by fire. You can take your body elsewhere and may change its outward appearance, but it makes no difference to your inner-being. Keep up with our poetry and music, Babu, and be good wherever you are."

Dadaji's words were reaching me like drops of water to a thirsty man.

"Just remember one thing for me, Babu. In London, you have a different social system and family values. But remember that your wife is like my daughter, even if I shall probably never see her. If you ever have any disagreement, think about it as if it was your mistake and your shortcoming. I know that you are a little strong in the head but remember that she is the mother of your children! You do remember what *Geeta* has taught us, don't you? Always try to say "Yes" to her and see if you can accommodate her wishes in what you do. Once we say someone is ours, we must always seek to reach a compromise with them, Yes?"

This was to be our last meeting. Dadaji passed away after some eight months.

Once my daughter asked me,

"Babbo, my friends have relatives and so many friends of the family. Where are your people?"

Dadaji was one of my people. I wished for once that God could give me an instant power of expression. I could then have crossed the generation gap and broken out of the time warp around me and told her about Dadaji in a way she could have understood!

7
Sulu

Sulu was a girl I first met at the age of five, when she was some seven years old. She was the niece of a rich man, who lived in a two-storeyed mansion in the neighbourhood. He was a generous man with a large family. His sister, Sulu's mother, was married to an artist from a family with an estate in an outlying district. Sulu and her older sister were both very pretty. They took after their aunt Heerabai, who was married to a nobleman. I never saw her in her young days but people used to compare any sweet-looking girl with her and ask,

"She is not as beautiful as Heerabai, is she?"

No one could ever be as gorgeous as Heerabai in her prime, but even a comparison with her was a great compliment.

All seemed well for a while until something rather strange happened. It was quite unexpected for that time, to say the least. One day, Sulu's mother was sent packing to her brother's house, with all her belongings and little Sulu. It came as a shock and no one knew exactly why it had happened. The rumours were plentiful. Some people thought that Sulu's father suspected that his wife was having an affair. This could not have been true. Apart from the fact that Sulu's mother was a kind and religious lady, no one in that sort of family resorted to such extreme measures. Such people were more likely to hush up the matter and save the family reputation. The other reason was that Sulu's father saw divine light and he had invited a Guru to stay with him. The Guru advised him to get rid of the worldly ties and devote his life to worshipping Lord Krishna. Sulu's elder sister was sixteen. Her marriage was arranged and got out of the way a few months earlier. The other two female members of the family had to be out of the house as the Guru had wished.

The Guru was a follower of *Premamarga*, one of the ways of expressing devotion among the worshippers of Krishna. (*Marga* in Sanskrit means "way" and *Prem* means "love".) The other ways included *Bhaktimarga*, which was common and involved prayers, fasting, etc. Devotees of *Premamarga* would express their love for the God through songs and dances with colourful costumes. Some unbelievers thought that the devotees were transsexuals. I did not believe in this and I knew that Sulu's father certainly had no such tendencies.

One morning, Sulu's uncle brought her to the courtyard in front of our house, where a few children were playing. He was well respected among the old and young alike. The children stopped playing and came near him.

"Look here, children! This is Sulu. Would you let her play with you please?"

The children were playing some simple games like marbles and a version of cricket with a soft rubber ball. Her uncle soon left but Sulu stood where she was. She took a good look around, with a finger close to her lips and just touching her teeth.

She was quite a spectacle in her red frock and her fair skin showing a healthy reddish colour on her cheeks in the bright sun. Her hair was a bit untidy and showed just a hint of curl close to the brow. I remember that her forehead was slightly moist with perspiration, like a few drops of dew on rose petals. This had been a standard feature on her face, which I always felt she should never wipe out!

She kept watching for a few moments, taking a stock of the children. Perhaps the games and the players did not appeal to her. Perhaps she would not rush into anything but play hard to get! Suddenly she saw me in the veranda and ran with the speed and grace of a young tigress.

"Hey, why are you sitting like a Ganapati on your own? What is your name, anyway?"

At the age of five, I was rather weak and not sociable. I was worried that the children would bully me. When I ventured to join them once, I was so bad with the game of marbles that they did not really want me any longer. I could read a little and preferred to be by myself on the veranda with my book. I used to sit on a wooden bench with my legs up near my chest. This might have made me look like the God *Ganapati*, the God of wisdom, well known for his large belly and the head of an elephant.

Sulu started talking and I was simply mesmerized. I never expected someone as agile and pretty as her to take any interest in me. She grabbed me by my hand and pulled me away from my seat. She took my book away, snatched a bat from a boy's hand and said,

"Come on, let's play!"

This little episode transformed my childhood, once and for all. Thereafter, I would wish that she could come down to play with me every afternoon. I would wait for her on the veranda after school, like a thirsty man waits for a drink. On some rare occasions, I would become engrossed in reading a book and she came without my seeing her first. She would tiptoe to my seat, touch my feet first and then my knees, and say a mock prayer as if I was *Ganapati*. Everyone would laugh but she said a sharp word or two to tell them off.

I soon developed some skills in the game of marbles and I could do some spin-bowling with the soft ball. I was a desirable playmate in a short time and even played in the local soft-ball cricket team. Sulu was my mentor and came to watch the game sometimes.

Some five years later, I was bowling in a friendly game. The ball must have hit a stone cropping up from the ground and it turned sharply. The batsman was out and his fellow team-members were annoyed. Contrary to all the rules of proper cricket, we decided to dig out the offending piece of stone straight away. I started to dig around it with a large pointed stone and Sulu was removing the soil. Then she wanted to dig and asked me to clear the soil. The opponents were getting impatient. Suddenly, she turned to tell someone to shut up and I was distracted too. Before anyone realised what might have happened, I gave a loud cry and clenched the palm and fingers of my left hand. The central finger was actually shattered above the first joint and my shirt was red with blood. A neighbour rushed me to the doctor and he stitched back the skin as much as he could.

I stayed in bed for two days and Sulu kept me company as often as she could. I saw a shadow of such genuine sorrow over her lovely face that I could not bear to see it, even in my own state of suffering. She would gently stroke my injured hand, believing that it would heal quickly in that way. I wished sincerely that she was wrong for once and my finger should not heal so quickly. I could then stay in bed and she would sit next to me and stroke my hand gently for a long time. My wish must have been granted partially! The tip of my finger has remained deformed as a permanent feature of my left hand, to remind me of the incident as long as I live!

She was not much good at studying and barely got through every school year. Thanks to my favourite class teacher, my mother's friend, I had a double promotion in the primary school. As a result, we were at the same stage of schooling. She would come to me for help sometimes but I could not really help her. I could understand the subjects but teaching someone else was well beyond me. She would end up saying that it was fair enough and she was happy with me being so very clever. I was not all that clever but I got the taste of feminine support at a very early stage!

She had a natural gift as a story teller. She specialised in ghost stories and they were really weird ones. I cannot remember them all but they used to send a shiver down my spine in those days. The ghosts were different, depending on the dead person and the way he or she died. Munja was a specially fierce type of ghosts. If a Brahmin boy were to die before the ceremony called Munj, to present him with a holy thread round his shoulder, his role in this world would remain unfulfilled. Instead of going to heaven, therefore, he would turn into a Munja ghost. (This ceremony signifies the conversion of a boy into a real Brahmin adult, comparable with the "confirmation" ceremony in Christian religion.)

A Munja ghost would be blind and it would walk along narrow paths keeping his hands moving horizontally in a scissor-like movement. Any boy with his height above a certain limit, who happened to be walking on the same path, would have his head chopped off! It seemed that Munjas would not hurt the girls, since they had a supernatural perception even if they appeared to be blind. This helped a lot, otherwise all girls in the neighbourhood would have refused to go to school! Sulu varied the safe limit as the time went by and, miraculously, my height was always below the limit. I had noticed some taller boys had retained the habit of walking with a stoop even in their adulthood. This might have been the result of having to keep below the "Munja limit" in their childhood, when walking after dark in narrow alleyways.

On my way to the school, I had to pass through a narrow lane and there was a big Banyan tree. Sulu's ghosts lived there. Some lived inside the hollow of the tree trunk. Some had their feet with toes pointing the wrong way round, towards the back, so that they could hang themselves on branches of trees, upside down like bats. They were either transparent or they could become very minute during the day and become large again after midnight. Until sunrise, the narrow lane was not safe. I believed her so much that, at one stage, I dared to ask uncle Hari to give me a holy thread like a Brahmin. He did oblige and on my way to school on some dark mornings, I used to hold the little knot of the thread between the tips of my fingers in my right hand. With this knot held this way and a chant of *"Rama, Rama"*, I must have been protected from all sorts of ghosts, large and small. Needless to say that these tips were given to me in private by my darling lady-protector. She was convinced that I had to be saved so that I would survive and succeed in life for her sake. Perhaps I did not quite fulfil her expectations but I remained unscathed and the ghosts kept well away from me!

Her stories about her uncle's wealth were strange. According to the versions she had heard, her mother's father had only a hardware shop at one time in a far away suburb. One evening, a visitor came to his house, carrying only a bundle of clothes, and asked him for a glass of water and shelter for the night in his shed. He was ill and someone even saw that he was wounded but not bleeding. The visitor slept a little and asked Sulu's grandfather a favour, later in the night at about eleven o'clock. He wanted some transport to go to the nearby village where he lived. The old man grudgingly obliged and they set off in a bullock cart. The visitor was quiet until they had travelled for about an hour. He then got up suddenly and wanted to urinate. He disappeared behind a bush and no one saw him again. He left his bundle behind, which contained jewelry in diamonds and gold. Sulu's grandfather barely saw him jump out of the bullock cart and, strangely enough, he thought his feet were back to front! He was a ghost of a robber, who had to return to his tree at midnight to hang himself upside down! Obviously, there were no police and detectives at that time and no one had reported any robbery in that area. Sulu's grandfather wisely kept the whole thing as a secret. He used the money as a capital to expand his hardware business. Success begot success thereafter and the family became very rich.

Sulu's uncle came to know about this version of his family fortune and dismissed it as a fiction. Of course, he was right. He scolded his errant niece for telling such stories.

She was not her uncle's favourite niece, anyway. By the time she was sixteen, he started worrying about her marriage. He talked about the problems he might have in finding a suitable match for her. Her father was not really interested in this and his efforts would perhaps have been counterproductive. Her uncle could use his own influence and money to find a suitable young man but it would not be easy. I was too young at fourteen to understand these problems. Even if I were to be four years older, the difference in the family status would have ruled me out. Again, I was too straight-forward to do something silly and cause any distress for both families.

Sulu often chided me for being too thoughtful. She put it down to my study of mathematics and physics. She often ridiculed my interest in geometry. She said that the science was useless for application in real life since there were no straight lines in human behaviour. She often taunted me this way and she was right.

"Why can't you be a little less predictable and stop thinking too much about so many things?"

She often asked me this question. She was always so convincing, smiling even when she told me off. Her face looked always pleasantly cool, perhaps helped by the hint of moisture on her forehead. She had measured me to the last millimetre and I wished I could have listened to her more carefully. I was, however, born to maintain the yoke of reasonableness on my shoulders for ever and I was destined to miss out happy and carefree moments on a number of occasions.

In 1955, I passed my school final with distinction and I stood first in the school. I got a number of prizes, which pleased everyone. Only uncle Hari was not fully satisfied. He expected me to be among the first twenty in the State of fifty million people and he would then have helped me to get a scholarship that would have taken me eventually to England for higher studies. Never mind, I said to myself at that time!

Sulu failed in her school final examination but she was overjoyed for me. School certificates did not mean much to her, she used to say. After a week or two, she came rushing to me and told me about the arrival of her old aunt Heerabai at her uncle's place. Her aunt wanted to see me and Sulu pleaded with me to see her. Heerabai had known about me as uncle Hari's nephew. Apparently, she had a very high opinion of my uncle and she was impressed by his foreign travels, his composure like a European, etc. I did not really want to see the grand old lady but I could not refuse anything Sulu asked me to do.

I went upstairs to the palatial sitting room. Heerabai was seated among a few other people, like a Lady Mayor, with her gold necklaces shining like the regalia. Her sari was among one of the most expensive types made with real silk and with real gold thread woven into the borders. She looked so grand that I had to make a real effort to be calm and not to be overawed. She called me and gave me one of her regal smiles.

"I have heard so much about you from your uncle Hari. Did you not manage to get second class after all? Bad luck, son. I am sure your father will find you some suitable training and a job."

I don't remember how I could take the shock and stay on my feet. This good lady had no education beyond reading and writing Marathi as such. She would also not know much about the efforts required to succeed in my examination. There was some apparent loss of accuracy in her interpretation of my uncle's narration about his disappointment that I was not in the top twenty in the State! Her misunderstanding perhaps suited her evaluation of limits for a boy of my background. She might have really believed that I would do very well if I could get a second class.

I was naughty for once and I apologized that I should have disappointed her by not getting the second class. The other people looked shocked but they remained speechless, as no one would dare to correct the great lady for my sake. I withdrew with outward calmness, but with my mind in a turmoil and my heart wounded by the insult. I made my way out through the back-rooms, using a short-cut to the exit from the mansion.

As I was passing through one of the empty rooms, I felt a gentle touch on my back, followed by a hushed voice. It was Sulu with tears in her eyes and a shadow of indignation on her gorgeous face. She gripped my hand and drew herself close to me. I saw the moist forehead from such close distance for the first time. Her silky hair touched my chin and I happened to touch her throbbing breast. I withdrew my hand and put it around her to draw her in a light embrace,

"What is the matter, Sulu?"

I asked her in a low voice, trying to comfort her. She caressed my face and kept still in my arms. After a few moments, she raised her eyes, kissed me gently and withdrew. She had said everything without uttering a single word!

Sulu was married after six months to the brother-in-law of her uncle's daughter. I did two years of college and went away from Mumbai for studying engineering. I saw Sulu a number of times but the meetings were casual. I had kept my most precious memories of her stored in the depth of my being. Nothing else should happen between us any more that could risk my treasured moments.

By the time I left Mumbai for England, Sulu was the mother of two girls, twelve and ten years old. She had lost the sparkle in her eyes by that

time but she had become every
inch a responsible mother and
wife.

I returned to Mumbai for my
first visit in 1974. Sulu was a
grandmother at the age of thirty-
six. She looked as pleasant as ever
but her hair showed some grey
streaks. She had aged faster than
others. She looked like a bird
confined to a large cage, where it
can move around freely but knows
the limits. She had become a

Sulu

caring housewife and, perhaps, the need to be consistently disciplined had
taken its toll.

Sulu and my wife met in 1979 during my second visit to Mumbai. Sulu
treated my wife as if she knew her. Perhaps she knew me so well that she
could judge what my wife would be like, in spite of the differences in their
origins and backgrounds. She was right in her judgement, as always! I was
delighted to see that the two girls I cared for were so good to each other.
My wife was overwhelmed with Sulu's extraordinary kindness towards
our daughter. I felt that perhaps she was content that her Babu was all
right after all!

Sulu passed away in 1989. She was so young, just fifty-one! I read her
obituary in the monthly magazine produced by our local club. She was
called a loving wife and mother. Of course, she must have been all right in
both these roles. I am not sure, however, whether anyone really knew how
full of life she was and what a natural person she was. I had heard a comment
made by a "so-called" educated person about her lack of formal education.
Her instincts were so good that she did not need any schooling.

What else could they say or write about Sulu, other than that permitted
by ordinary perception? I was among the few privileged to know her better
than that!

8
Eric

*E*ric was a Catholic, born and brought up in Mumbai. In fact, his family roots were in Mumbai, like many other Catholics I knew personally. Their forefathers were among the original Mumbai residents and this was the common link between us. My mother used to like Eric very much. He was one of my close friends in my youth, despite the difference in our religions.

Eric

Forefathers of the majority of Catholics in Mumbai belonged to the local Hindu community in the sixteenth century. This was the time when the Portuguese came to the West Coast of India. The local historical stories of that period include various records of activities of the Portuguese missionaries. They were told by their rulers that they should not do anything that might displease the natives. They took interest in the plight of the lower castes, gave them work and tried to convert them into Christians by force or by financial inducements. The upper castes were apparently too naive to realise the consequences of these tactics. The missionaries found another way of mass conversion, by pure chance, which must have easily been far more effective than coercion using force or financial incentives.

One day, a farmer drew water from his well as usual for household purposes. The bucket brought up a loaf of bread, which was probably dropped there by a bird. As luck would have it, a Hindu priest was passing by. He saw the bread and ordered the farmer to throw the water away. The priest commanded that the farmer must not to use the well any longer, until a religious ceremony was carried out to bless it and make the water acceptable to Hindus again. Bread was known to be the symbol of Christ's flesh used in Christian rituals. Hindus also believed that the Christian bakers made bread using some animal fat. The news of this little episode spread very fast.

The next day, pieces of bread were found in a number of wells, particularly in the poorer areas. Agents of Portuguese priests were thought to be responsible for this. The plot seemed to include dropping loaves of bread in the wells and wait until the water from such wells was used by the unsuspecting owner's family, without noticing the bread. Some strong armed people would soon announce the fate of the family that they were not Hindus any longer. This had a devastating effect on many illiterate communities. It took some time for the Hindu religious leaders to react. In the end, mass conversion was halted by introducing a simple procedure involving some prayers to negate the effect of bread on the well and the water. However, those who were "converted" earlier had to remain Christians. A few decades later, some pragmatic Hindu pundits devised a purification campaign but it did not have any significant effect.

In many areas, the new Christians continued to follow the traditional Hindu worships in private. They would go to church on Sundays but their culture did not change for all practical purposes. On the other hand, some churches became popular with Hindus, for example, Mount Mary in North Mumbai became known to Hindus as "Mount Mauli" meaning "Mother on the hill". Contrary to the principles of Christianity, people used to offer various objects to the shrine, so that their wishes might be granted. Tiny models of parts of the human body, hands or legs or ears, could be offered with the hope that the "Mother-Goddess" would bless the devotee and cure the ailment in those parts of his or her body. These models were made in wax, or brass or even silver, depending on what one could afford.

I met Eric in 1957 at Ahmedabad, where both of us were admitted for a degree course in Civil Engineering. The college was truly cosmopolitan, with students from many Indian cities. Some of the students came from as afar as Africa, Nepal and Goa. (Goa was a Portuguese Colony at that time but it was taken over by India within a few years.) Non-resident students stayed in the college hostel or hired private rooms if they wished. Eric and I shared a room with a Goan student. This boy, Aneel, was a Hindu but considered himself to be a foreigner. He would gang up with other Goans and Africans. They were rather snobbish and indulged in vitriolic criticism of Indians and Marathi people. To his eternal credit, Eric used to associate himself with us. He could have won their favour as a Christian, as some other Christian boys did, but Eric was a Bombaywallah! This formed a strong bond between us, which was to last for many years.

Eric was a gifted hockey player, an outside-right forward player with great skills and speed to go past the defenders. As it happened, Goans and Africans formed a large part of the sports contingent, particularly the hockey and football teams. They were more athletic and stronger than the local Gujarati boys, who were not interested in such sports, anyway.

I had no talent as far as outdoor sports were concerned. In 1957, I weighed about six stones (38 kg) and my height was five feet two inches (156 cm). Eric was much taller and he would stand at the top end of the line-up at physical training sessions. I was near the bottom end. I must have been a late developer. After three years of life in Ahmedabad, my weight was eight stones (51 kg) and my height became nearly five feet nine inches (175 cm).

Eric's sporting prowess soon won over the other sportsmen. I acquired an important role as their supporter and honorary team manager. This task included functions ranging from arranging friendly matches to taking care of their belongings during the games. It was gratifying to hear the mellowed comments from Aneel and his cronies that we Bombaywallahs were not so bad after all!

My association with these people induced me to take part in some sport. I could manage only table tennis and I did rather well at the college tournaments. Eric was a natural with all ball games. We used to practise together after everyone had left the hall, sometimes at eleven o'clock in the night. This did not go down well with the Rector, when he saw us during his late night walk. However, we were both good boys and he let us off with a mild rebuke.

Eric came to see my mother during the college vacations. He would sit on the floor and eat, just like us. By the time we passed our degree examinations, he had almost become one of the family! We tried hard to find a job together. We were called for an interview by the same firm. We succeeded and we started our training on the same day. Eric wanted to work on construction sites and I had decided to be a design engineer. Eric's grasp for the subject and his capacity to do hard work was phenomenal. Within three years, he was appointed as an assistant resident engineer on a medium-size construction project.

As a coincidence, he was once posted on the site of a project, for which I had worked on the design and drawings. My head of the section, Mirzasaab, used to admire our teamwork and even enjoy our arguments at meetings. We often faced each other from the opposite sides. I insisted that Eric should follow the drawings and specifications strictly, while Eric tried to point out some discrepancies. Somehow, we always reached a compromise and learnt a lot from each other.

I remember the time when we went to a place in Central India to negotiate a contract with the Executive Engineer, one Mr Kand. He was a jolly fellow, with a large family, servants, etc. He probably formed a good opinion about the two of us and everything went very smoothly. He often liked to have informal meetings at his residence and sorted out a number of things off the record. I was really impressed with this technique.

He had a peculiar but agreeable sense of humour. As soon as the guests arrived and sat down, he would call his servant and tell him to get refreshment, tea or soft drinks according to the time of the day. He would ask his servant,

"Ramu, how many plates do we need?"

Ramu had to count the number of people and increase it by one. If Ramu failed to answer correctly, he was told off using the spiciest vernacular terms! Mr Kand had a theory that some unexpected person would invariably come late and there should always be a plate ready for the latecomer! Mr Kand was right on most occasions. Very rarely have I seen two latecomers or none at all! This must seem contradictory to the customs in Europe. However, Mr Kand was an Indian from Central India, the heart of the country, and his method seemed to work in his province.

Mr Kand gave us many concessions and the firm had a profitable contract. Eric suspected that Mr Kand had an ulterior motive and he saw me as a prospective son-in-law. Perhaps I was too much of a professional to mix business with anything else. Perhaps I was unlucky, because Mr Kand had very charming daughters. However, I believe that Eric was wrong. Although Mr Kand's hospitality was genuine, he did very well for his

Department by getting a good job done for the right price and by employing a good quality firm. Eric, however, told my mother about the episode and caused me some embarrassment for a while!

I used to visit Eric's work-sites occasionally as a head-office quality control officer. Eric knew how to manage work-force, with the right mixture of firmness and compassion. I was always regarded and treated well as Ericsaab's friend. However, on one occasion, I had an experience that is hard to forget.

This project had two sections and Eric was in charge of one of them. The other section had a few European supervisors, even after some eighteen years of the end of British Raj. During my round of this section, I saw a young man working on concreting and his waterproof shoes were torn. This was contrary to the health and safety regulations and I asked his foreman to get him a new pair. Within a short time, a fat red-faced Irishman came growling at me,

"Who the f*** you think you are? Keep your head-office ideas to yourself and don't meddle with the workers. You don't know these little thieves. These guys get new shoes and sell the old ones on the black market."

I could not match the man's vocabulary. I thought, however, that I convinced him about my authority and that I was right in what I did. As I was leaving the site that evening, a six foot tall Sikh crane-driver came to me and said,

"I saw what happened, Babusaab! That Irish pig is a real bastard. He gets bribes from all the suppliers and he has grown fat on a number of underhand deals."

I pleaded with him that I did not really want to know this. But he went on,

"Saab, he was once rude to Ericsaab and abused him for using the telephone for too long. Ericsaab threw the telephone at him and told him to f*** off. That's what he deserves! Saab, we know the two of you very well. You shouldn't have to put up with such insults. Tomorrow, one of us will go for him and drop a crane-bucket on his head!"

I was petrified with the thought of seeing the fat-bellied foreman flat on his back and his blood spilt all over the place. One thing was certain that the Sikhs would never joke! The man meant what he said and I had to calm him down. I quoted some Sanskrit verses to him meaning that my soul was indestructible and impervious to any insults. I also pleaded with him that the foreman must have been brought up badly and that one could not sink to the level of causing him injuries. I knew that the Sikh had been a crane-driver for years and he could not be worried about the law, etc.

In the end, the crane-driver restrained himself and the Irishman lived. He went back to his country, as his liver problem grew worse with the consumption of free illicit liquor he got from the tradesmen.

Eric and I kept in touch even after Eric left the firm and found a better job elsewhere. We had made a deal that one would attend the full ceremony when the other got married. Eric beat me to it. He married a beautiful girl from Panjim in Goa. I had a two-week leave and enjoyed the full treatment of Goan hospitality.

Within two years of his marriage, Eric was asked to work on the northern frontier of India on a large road building scheme. This was a consequence of the conflict with China. As the bad luck would have it, I lost my job as a result of the Government cut-back on other building projects. Our firm was reduced by half and I was a part of the half that had to leave. I came to England while Eric was near the Himalayas.

One day I got a letter from my mother and the sad news about Eric. He was the victim of a land-mine explosion. For me, it was a death of a soldier. He might have died as a Christian, but he could well have been one of our own community, descendant of the warrior race from Rajputana.

9
Mirzasaab

*M*irza Hassan or Mirzasaab was my senior colleague for some five years. He was a devout Muslim and a scholar in Urdu poetry. He was tall, slim and fair-skinned, a Nawab or an aristocrat in the real meaning of the word. His family history could be traced back to the seventeenth century. One of his ancestors had served under a Muslim ruler of a province in Maharashtra, the Shah of Vijapoor. After the demise of Muslim rule, part of his family settled near Poona and the others went to Hyderabad in south India, the State where Nizam

Mirzasaab

ruled at one time. Mirzasaab had studied at Poona University and moved to Mumbai for work. As far as he was concerned, he belonged to Mumbai.

In 1960, I was a new boy in a firm full of foreign-trained Indian engineers and with some Britons as group leaders. Among the genuine Indian engineers, Mirzasaab was the brightest rising star. He had passed the prestigious entrance examination for membership of the Institution of Structural Engineers, at the first attempt and with a prize for the highest marks. He took this examination to prove a point to one of the Englishmen, who had passed a casual remark about the Indian Universities. He was not aware of the high standard at the University of Poona. He also did not know that a true blood Poona University student would never tolerate any criticism of his *Alma Mater.* Mirzasaab was no exception and this made him popular among the Marathi staff, although his mother-tongue was Urdu and he could not speak Marathi very well.

As a fresh local graduate, I was at the bottom of the ladder. For the first few months, I had to practise drawing as a part of our training. For trainees earmarked for construction work, like my friend Eric, this took about six months. For design office trainees, training in drawing was for a longer period and it was followed by some quantity-surveying. After about one year of such training, one could expect to get some design work. Mirzasaab was rather high-up in the hierarchy and I did not get to speak with him for the first six months.

The training was no bed of roses and often resembled the old-fashioned army training. The chief draftsman, Ramayya, was a big, dark South Indian fellow, in the sergeant-major mould. He was a self-made man of the old school, with good experience but without any formal education. He was a disciplinarian, who believed that the best training required harsh words. His reference to the shortcomings of college education was invariably sarcastic. It was often meant to humiliate the would-be design engineers. Construction trainees like Eric got off lightly. Eric escaped from Ramayya's camp within some five months or so. On the contrary, I was an easy target for him, although I could manfully carry on with my work and ignored his harsh remarks.

One afternoon, the man must have been in a real foul mood and picked on me for no real reason. He told me that my drawing was all wrong, without telling me the reasons for his displeasure. It was one of the worst humiliating experiences for me. Only the respect for grey hair in my nature stopped me from retaliating. Instead, I decided that I should work late in the evening and see if anything was really wrong with my task, when all was quiet in the office.

In my sombre state of mind, I did not realise that Mirzasaab was standing close to my table. He must have finished a late meeting with someone in the building and returned to collect his briefcase before going home.

"What is the matter, Babu? You haven't had an argument with your parents, have you?"

He asked me in his cheerful voice.

I told him the reason for my staying behind. He looked very impressed.

"That's the spirit, young man. If someone says you are wrong, don't take it lying down. Don't worry who the chappy is. Do make absolutely sure that your work is all correct. If you are confident that you are in the right, say so loudly and clearly."

He glanced at my drawing and picked up the problem within minutes. The problem was with the drawing that Ramayya had given me as the starting point and not with my own work. I could not see it myself, partly due to my inexperience and partly because I could not believe that an experienced man like Ramayya could make such mistakes.

I was relieved and I thanked Mirzasaab.

"Don't just thank me, Babu. Go home now and have a good night's sleep. Come back in the morning and tell the old man firmly, without any fear, that it was his fault. Remember, I shall be watching you!"

He gave me a lift in his car and asked me a few simple questions. He suggested that I might wish to consider working in his group. If I wished, he would try to arrange it, although he couldn't promise anything straight away. The thought of working with Mirzasaab filled me with happiness and I really slept well that night!

Next morning, my colleagues saw something that they were to remember for years to come. I saw Ramayya come in and waited for him to sit down. I approached him but he growled at me saying that he was too busy and he had no time for me that morning.

"You shall have time for me and you shall have it now!"

I demanded. I could feel the atmosphere of mild disbelief all around me. But the worm had turned! I told Ramayya what the problem was, in a calm but firm voice. I put it to him clearly that he should have provided me with correct details in the first place. He tried to bamboozle me with some irrelevant points and dismiss me rather brashly. But I had taken a grip on him like a bulldog and didn't let go. In the end, he murmured something to the effect that it was fair enough and gave me another job.

I was working with Mirzasaab within a week, after he had sorted it out with the boss, the chief engineer. The boss had a report of my encounter with Ramayya already. It seemed to have amused him and perhaps convinced him that, if I could face Ramayya so well, I must be ready for a proper engineer's work.

The first few years of my career were the happiest. When Mirzasaab, Eric and I happened to work together, it was like a unique tri-colour combination of different minds. Mirzasaab was a hard taskmaster and a real no-nonsense fellow. He worshipped perfection, to the very best achievable limits and insisted that others do the same. He would not tolerate any sloppy designs and unjustifiable approximations. Some older engineers believed that they had considerable experience and that detailed study could be dispensed with, in the interest of speed. Mirzasaab was right, as the build-up of such approximations could lead to mistakes if the conditions for the previous project did not really apply to the new one and so on. He was indeed one of the finest civil engineers I have ever worked with.

Engineering was only one of the facets of his character. He really was very proficient in most things that interested him. I believe that he would apply his engineering principles to most other things. He knew that engineering was an approximation of physics and mathematics and not a pure science. Human life was very similar, but one had to operate within some rules based on the present day circumstances, judgement and statistics, for all their worth.

He was a devoted Muslim but he had very clear views on the religion, based on fundamental principles. He would often express his regrets about misinterpretations of the religious doctrines, which he had studied very carefully. For example, women had far more rights than the existing practice would permit, particularly in the field of education, according to the basic Muslim principles.

He hated blind application of arbitrary and approximate rules developed by engineering codes of practice. He compared them with the doctrines modified by selfish kings and plutocrats, who would even enforce changes in the religious practice to justify their sinful actions. I often heard his discourses over tea and lunch. I would point out that Hindu religion had also suffered deviations from the basic principles. He would laugh and say that most of the problems of the world would disappear if good engineers could be religious leaders or even rule the world. After all, structures would not be good or bad as a direct result of what the codes say. The application was more important than the rules, which the engineers could do better than the professional politicians. However, the thought of engineers succeeding in politics must seem a far-fetched idea, since the two professions are known to be too dissimilar to mix. Engineering deals with materials and elements with properties and response to actions within some predictable range. The same cannot be said with politics dealing with human behaviour, however, which often has a wide and unreliable range.

For someone meeting him for the first time, Mirzasaab would appear to be rather harsh. It took time to know him well. When he knew you and you were frank and honest with him, he was the best person to have on your side. I found him a good role model of what a Marathi saint called a *Vishnudas* (disciple of *Vishnu*, the most revered God of Hindus). A *Vishnudas* should have the strength of mind to sustain any calamity. On certain occasions, however, he should be as soft in the heart as if it were made of wax. A *Vishnudas* would give everything he has to someone in distress but he would not hesitate hitting an oppressor on his head, if it came to that.

The softness of Mirzasaab's heart was most visible when he was at his home with his son. His wife was like a Mughal princess, beautiful and composed. To listen to the couple converse in Urdu was an ultimate linguistic experience. It would be impossible to be impolite if one could speak Urdu correctly. Only intimate family members could address each other in the second person form *Tum*. Everyone else had to use the respectful way using a pronoun in the third person *Aap* just like the Italian pronoun *Lei*.

His apparent harshness could occasionally disappear even outside his home, when he would hum an Urdu couplet. The Urdu language and Sanskrit have a remarkably common and traditional form of poetry, where a poet must express deep feelings in two lines of a verse. It would come out at the moment of inspiration or on an occasion that might have touched his heart. However, such poets were no ordinary writers but they spent their lives in studying the language. A poet would master the language so thoroughly that the words could emerge naturally when the right moment arrived, to suit the expression of his feelings.

Mirzasaab would not sing to an audience but a few of us were privileged to hear his rendition of a couplet or two, on rare occasions. The words were beautiful, rendered with the correct musical embellishment, just the way the poet would have wanted to express his feeling. Among his fans besides me, was a peon, *Sepoy* Dattaram as everyone called him. He would just listen to an occasional mini-concert, while he operated his machine for copying drawings outside our office. In all this, decorum was observed to the full. I nodded approvingly and say something in a low voice like *"Wah-wah, Bahot Khoob"*. (Bravo, well done!) Dattaram just smiled under his moustache and put his hands together without making any clapping sound.

The most remarkable scene, which has remained in my memory for ever, took place at the entrance of our washroom. (We had separate rooms, some for washing hands and cups only and some with toilets and washbasins.) It was just after the beginning of lunch-time and most people had gone away, except those who would have packed lunch at their desk. All was quiet and Mirzasaab had gone to the washroom to wash his hands before starting his lunch. The door was partly open and he began humming a tune, in a low voice first and then a little louder. It was a popular song about the gratitude of the poet towards his friends. I was outside in the corridor and I saw Dattaram close to the door of the washroom but out of Mirzasaab's sight. He was nodding like a devotee with his eyes closed, his hands clapping very gently and keeping with the rhythm of the song. He had an expression of happiness on his face that money could not buy! It was a rare and heart-warming sight, where the difference between the master and the servant had evaporated in the heavenly atmosphere filled with music.

Although the role-reversal involved an entertainer as a Muslim prince, entertaining a Hindu servant, this was most akin to any scene from Hindu mythology. Our Hindu images of Gods, particularly in the province of Maharashtra, are remarkably egalitarian. We have many stories about the God becoming the servant of any genuine devotee. The best-loved temple in Maharashtra is that of the image of God as *Vithoba*, who once came with his Goddess wife to visit a young devotee. The young man was serving his parents at that time, which was his first duty. He could not attend the visitors straight away. Instead, he slid a couple of bricks towards the visitors, for them to stand on. The God and the Goddess are represented as a sculpture in the temple of *Vithoba, Vit* being the word for a brick in Marathi.

In another case, the God saved a devotee by becoming an untouchable servant and went to the Mughal king to deliver the taxes, when the devotee could not do so himself. This must come across as a symbol of slave mentality in the eighteenth century Maharashtra but it has to be understood for the implied sentiments and in the right context.

Mirzasaab would pray five times a day but did not consider that he was more devout as a Muslim than those who could not manage to pray so many times. He used to love the story of a proud Indian saint who claimed to be the best devotee of the God, as he chanted the God's name and prayed all the time. The God came in his dreams one day and asked him to take a bowl filled with oil up to the brim to a farmer in the next village and warned him not to spill a single drop. Next day the God came again in the saint's dream and asked him about his trip. The saint said that he had accomplished the mission. But when the God asked him whether he kept chanting His name during the journey, the saint felt ashamed. He could not chant the God's name and simultaneously concentrate on carrying the bowl of oil without spilling any drop. The God told him that the farmer in the next village prayed twice a day, in spite of his worries about the rain, the crop, the wife's health and his children. The saint had his eyes opened and he no longer boasted about his devotion to the God.

Mirzasaab had some wonderful principles of his own. He believed in charity and generosity, but only up to a limit. He would often say that it would be all right to give some of your food to a fellow at your table but you should never give up your seat at the table. He was also a great advocate of keeping one's eye on the long term goal and not expending too much energy on trivial matters. He had adopted a European way of thinking about these matters and not the traditional Indian way advocating death for one's principles and no compromise even on insignificant matters. Perhaps as a keen Contract Bridge player, Mirzasaab believed in winning the final match and not just a rubber.

One of our Indian Directors, Mr Juhukar, was a brilliant man and should have been promoted to be the Managing Director. However, the Board decided to promote one of the last remaining European Directors. He would have retired within eighteen months and the promotion would have enhanced his pension. Mr Juhukar threatened to resign on principle and he achieved a hero's status. A staff meeting was held and Mirzasaab was the only person who begged Mr Juhukar to be patient and wait for a while.

Mr Juhukar

Some people had a doubt about Mirzasaab's integrity. I knew that he really wanted Mr Juhukar to stay, as he respected him so much. He pleaded with Mr Juhukar that he would get the job next time, anyway, and that he deserved it. The Board accepted Mr Juhukar's resignation and the European was in the post for just one year or so. Unfortunately, the post was given to another Indian, who would have been junior to Mr Juhukar.

Mirzasaab became most unhappy with this outcome. Apparently, the departing Europeans had stripped the assets of the firm and, one day, Mirzasaab was involved in a very unpleasant scene with the new Managing Director. We were all worried about this. Rumours about Mirzasaab getting the sack, or being asked to resign, were soon rife. Some hardworking engineers were sacked already out of spite, since they would not co-operate with the villains.

Mirzasaab must have belonged to the warrior race, the descendants of the Turks who had conquered India at the beginning of the second millennium. He knew instinctively that this might happen one day, following Mr Juhukar's departure. Like an engineer, he had foreseen the danger and a hazard and he had prepared his defence. There are various versions of the story but I shall tell the one I believe to be true.

Since no one had the courage to reprimand Mirzasaab on his own, they called him into a boardroom. This was an inquisition or an ambush, or both. The atmosphere in the office was tense. Mirzasaab came ten minutes later than the appointed time, immaculately dressed and humming a tune. I have never seen so many gaping faces with open mouths in a closed office! With a greeting to the left and a wave of hand to the right, he went to the boardroom.

About an hour later, he returned, a little tired but still smiling. All seemed to be all right in the end!

Later in the evening, he told me the whole story. He had obtained documented proof of embezzlement and dishonesty of the previous management, implicating the new Managing Director as well. He had thrown them to the wall, as he put it, and hung them on the hooks there. He had told them that he would take them to the court, unless they either reinstated or paid full compensation to each person they had sacked recently. They should let him work independently and allow him to choose his own team. He gave them one week to do all this.

A tense week passed and everything happened as Mirzasaab had asked.

Life was back to normal but without those who had been sacked earlier. They preferred to take their compensation and went to work elsewhere. Three out of the five engineers went to America.

After some months, Mirzasaab told me in confidence about his meeting with Mr Juhukar in connection with the crisis. Mr Juhukar had heard what Mirzasaab wanted to do but tried to persuade him to think otherwise. Mirzasaab could achieve his aim of beating the villains but they could get away with some fines and avoid jail sentences. They could then leave India and live happily on the money tucked away in their Swiss Bank Accounts. Mirzasaab's success would also mean closure of the firm and loss of livelihood for honest people like Sepoy Dattaram. These people would suffer and their families could be devastated.

Mirzasaab told me about the profound effect Mr Juhukar had on him. He had made up his mind to play his cards close to his chest like a poker player and he won. He did not tell me what he would have done if the villains had stuck to their guns. After all, what didn't happen could not be worth talking about!

Within a year or so, the effects of Chinese conflict were apparent on the Indian construction industry. I had just passed my examination that would make me a member of the Institution of Structural Engineers. I hoped to get a pay increase and perhaps a promotion. Mirzasaab had a long chat with me and he gave me a strong hint that I should move to the contracts section if I could, instead of carrying on in the design office. There was a position there and the man in charge knew me. I went and saw him and explained to him what my hopes were.

I realised soon, as things stood at that time, that it was a mistake. The head of the contracts section was a shrewd man, who knew that I wanted to work on design of structures. He would have helped me with the transfer but he had to be sure of my will to work for him.

I stayed in the design office for six months more. One day, I got my notice or marching orders. This was the end of my career with the firm. I worked here and there for one year but without any real luck. In one case, I worked hard to produce a scheme but the person, who gave me the work, would not pay me. He said that the job was for a charity and I should treat this as an investment for the future! I spent three months without work and used to spend the days out of the house, in cinemas or even in bars. The only sensible thing I did was to apply for a visa to go to the USA or to the UK.

One morning, I got my UK visa. The American visa would have taken a little longer. I was in a terrible state. Our society is kind but it can appear to be cruel to a young man out of work. People would invariably think that something must be wrong with the young man.

Ironically, a dear friend suggested that I should marry his wife's sister. I could have then worked in one of the firms belonging to his businessman father-in-law. I could have become a manager of a hotel or a chicken farm. The girl could drive a car and I could have had a car and a furnished apartment. I could also start my own business. I had some money, given as a compensation by the firm, which was not such a bad sum. Decisions, decisions! I had to act soon, otherwise I would have gone mad.

I had the strong desire to remain a civil engineer, inspired by my uncle Hari earlier on. I was too proud, perhaps like my Kshatriya or warrior ancestors, who believed in earning their own living and who would not accept anything free. Perhaps I was a little silly and I thought too much, as Sulu used to say! However, I could not marry a girl from a family so much richer than mine. My friend's father-in-law was a kind and a truly generous man. But so what? He would have honoured my wish to keep my own independence, but my success would always be looked upon as a result of his influence. I spent some torrid time and, in the end, went to see Mirzasaab.

He was about to leave his job with the firm, having worked for certain years that would give him a good pension and a sizeable lump-sum. He would go to Hyderabad for ever. He listened to me carefully and declined to give me any advice.

"This is your life, my boy! You must sort it out."

He said quite clearly. Just as I was leaving, He said,

"Babu, think of the long game, whatever you do. Don't go for an easy option, attractive only in the short term. See what is most important to you and think carefully about those for whom you really care."

I knew what he was saying. I told my mother that I wanted to go to the UK. I wanted to be a civil engineer all my life. I would not do anything that would ever embarrass her. My mother understood me or perhaps she was fed up with me going around in such a state. I left Mumbai in search of work and came to London.

I met Mirzasaab again in 1974 in London. I was already married and we had a daughter by then. He was on his way back to Mumbai from his trip to the USA. He had visited his son, who lived in Miami, and wanted to have a tour around Europe before going back to Hyderabad. He came to see me at my house with his wife. He asked me if I was happy. He was very sweet with my wife and my little girl. He was mellowed a bit, I thought. He could not resist telling my wife about my early days, the marriage proposals I had and my plight before leaving Mumbai. Fortunately, I had already told her everything. He was surprised about our openness with each other and exclaimed in his old mischievous manner,

"You have both done very well, haven't you Babu? I am sure that you must have found one of the very few virgins in London and Anita must have found the only bachelor who had never slept with a woman before! I know I am right, my boy, and I am ready to bet ten thousand rupees."

I rolled over laughing. Anita blushed a little and so did his wife. I could not resist teaching a lesson to my one-time mentor and *Guru*.

"Mirzasaab, I am happy to let you keep your money, although you have lost the bet. I treat this as a token of my gratitude for all your generosity during my life in Mumbai. We are all square now, Yes?"

He did not quite accept his defeat openly. But I knew that I was on equal terms with him from that time onwards, which was a moment to savour!

Within a few years, his wife died and he went to Miami to live with his son. I had lost touch with him and I had no news about him until I met one of my ex-colleagues, who told me about his death in 1997. I shall be one of the many, who will treasure his memories for ever!

10
Doctor

*I*t was the beginning of my second
year as a student at the Ruparel
College in Mumbai, studying for my
Intermediate Science course. Some
of my school friends had joined the
same college and we studied
together during the first year. All of
us had done very well at our first
year examination. The first year
curriculum consisted of all science
subjects, Physics, Chemistry,
Mathematics and Biology. A student
had to decide whether to take
Mathematics, Group A, or Biology,
Group B, during the next year as his

Doctor

or her specialist subject. I had the highest marks in Mathematics and the
second highest in Biology. Professors from departments responsible for both
Groups were keen on my joining their Groups. I had made up my mind to be
a civil engineer and, therefore, my choice had to be Group A. One had to
have over 70% marks at the Intermediate Science examination with Group
A, as an essential entrance qualification for any branch of engineering studies,
either civil or mechanical or electrical. Similarly, such success with Group B
was required for those who wished to do medical or pharmaceutical studies.
One could choose either of the Groups and go for a degree of Bachelor of
Science. In those days, this was considered as a choice imposed on lesser
mortals! However, good careers were available for science graduates,
although not as good as those for doctors and engineers. My friends were
reasonably content with their results and a trifle jealous of the fact that I
could have chosen either of the Groups without any difficulty.

We were having our tea in the canteen during the recess and chatting about our future plans and about some of our fellow students, who were less than fortunate with their first year results. A smart young man, dressed far better than any of us, was at the next table. He looked more like a lecturer than a student. He was listening to our conversation with an expression on his face, as if amused by our reminiscing the experience during the first year at college and our congratulating each other for our good results. Perhaps, he was feeling a little forlorn and out of place in those surroundings.

I saw him again during the next break and we walked together to a table. He asked us if he could join us at the table. We were quite happy to have him. He introduced himself as Navin Shah. He was a Jain by religion and well off, we thought, judging by his expensive clothes, gold watch and gold-rimmed spectacles. He was offered a scholarship by an organisation of rich people from his community to study in America but he had to pass Intermediate Science examination with Group B to get it. He said that he had to leave his studies after completing his secondary school education. He seemed very bright and polite and a likeable sort. He paid us compliments on our success and we, in our turn, agreed to give him all help we could. He did not seem to attend classes regularly and often borrowed my notes. I became quite friendly with him, as we often travelled on the same train back home.

After about six months, we became very busy with our project work and I did not realise that Navin had not attended college for more than a week. I knew that he took gaps of a day or two occasionally but this was longer than usual. I went to the general office and asked if there was anything wrong with Navin. They told me that he had an accident and that he was in "Nair Hospital". I did not know much about the hospitals but this was a rather large one and the college had no other information like the ward number or the section of the hospital.

I wanted to go to see Navin but I did not see any way to find him and the hospital would not give any details unless I was a relative. I asked my father for his advice. Although my father did not care much about the details of my studies, he was moved to see my predicament and my urge to see my unfortunate college friend. He knew a worker in his textile mill, whose brother was an ambulance driver at the hospital. It must seem very odd and irregular now but, at that time, I was very happy when the ambulance driver agreed to escort me and search with me all the seven floors of the casualty wing of the hospital, where patients like Navin were treated. That is what I did, in the company of my escort. There were no lifts and we climbed up the stairs. We entered each floor at one end, looked carefully in the special rooms at that end and then checked the beds on the left and on the right in turn as we walked. We then left the floor at the other end, checked the special rooms there and went up the stair to examine the next floor.

Navin was in a special room on the fifth floor. He had one side of his face bandaged. He was pleasantly surprised to see me. My escort went out for an hour, leaving us alone. Navin could talk and move about without any discomfort. He rang the bell and a nurse came quickly.

"Is everything all right, Dr. Shah?"

She asked politely. Ignoring my surprise for a moment, Navin asked her to bring some tea. He soon put me out of my miseries and told me that he was a qualified physician in the Ayurvedic branch of medicine. He had studied in Bhopal, a city in the central part of India, where he could take an entrance examination after finishing secondary school. He was a house-surgeon in one of the leading Ayurvedic hospitals in Mumbai. His ambition was to go to America and do research in combining application of Ayurvedic remedies with western medicines. This could cure various medical conditions prevalent in the developing countries, more effectively and economically than using the expensive and imported western medicines on their own. He could go to America if he could finish the Intermediate Science course and some top-up tests, which were essential for admission to the American University. Navin had been promised a scholarship and he would have left for America during the next year, if all had gone smoothly.

All these plans were now in jeopardy. Navin was the victim of some racial attack as he was going home on foot after seeing a patient nearby. He told me that someone was hiding in a narrow alley-way and rushed at him, threw acid in his face and ran away. The police were making inquiries but to no avail. It seemed likely that this was a case of mistaken identity.

Time went by rather quickly while Navin was telling me his sad story. My escort returned after an hour and I promised Navin that I would come again after two days. Next time, I went with my sister instead of the kind ambulance driver. The nurse attending Navin could arrange for our visit, as she knew about our friendship and Navin was, after all, no ordinary patient. As a coincidence, Navin's wife had come at the same time, which was fortuitous because my sister felt at ease with the presence of another female. I remember Navin's wife as a very thin young lady of some twenty-three years of age. She spoke in a village accent, rather quickly and in a manner that showed her inexperience in meeting strangers. Navin did not behave particularly like a loving husband and, even in that condition, made fun of her and joked about her being a village girl. Her name was Renuka, a name from an Indian religious story, but Navin told us to call her Bayji. Bayji and my sister seemed to get on well and Bayji accepted us immediately as intimate friends of the family. With her, people were either strangers or part of the family and nothing in between! She must have been devoted to Navin and referred to him as Doctor, which is why we started using it as if it were his first name in place of Navin.

Doctor was soon released from the hospital. He rested for a short while but did not come back to the college. We met a few times afterwards but I was very deeply involved in my preparation for my examination, as my future depended on it. Within a few months, Doctor went to hospital again for some plastic surgery. I got my results and they were good enough for getting admission to a degree course in civil engineering. Doctor had a successful skin-transplant and his face looked much better. We met during my holidays before going to Ahmedabad. Doctor took his narrow escape from disaster as a new lease of life and concentrated on his practice. He soon bought a car and vowed to use it all the time. He would never go on foot anywhere again, however short the distance may be.

Doctor was a very religious man, an orthodox Jain. He prayed every morning for some forty minutes, with the same devotion as uncle Hari would read Geeta. He was a strict vegetarian. He would not touch any food after sunset. He detested smoking and drinking alcohol. He was enthusiastic about Ayurvedic medicine and tonics made out of fruit, nuts, raisins and bark and leaves of certain trees. His tooth paste was also Ayurvedic. He practised regularly some exercise, a simplified form of Yoga, and kept himself fit. He maintained that illness came principally because of an imbalance in the strength of various harmones in the body. He was disciplined in his ways to limits that were totally unattainable for me!

Within some six months of my leaving home for Ahmedabad, my mother suddenly became very ill. She had an acute pain at the back of her left shoulder and then she lost any use of her left arm. She could not move without help. For an active lady like her, it was a psychological blow as well as a physical illness. We had our own family doctor, a jolly fellow and a good doctor as far as normal illness and routine problems were concerned. He came to see my mother and expressed a grave concern. He said that she should be taken to the hospital immediately and treated by a specialist. It was too much for my sister to bear and she was truly distraught. As soon as our family doctor had left, there was all gloom in our household. Our father was not much of any help and there was literally no one my sister could turn to at that time. Fortunately, she remembered about our Doctor. She went to a public phone some five hundred yards away and called to say just a few words,

"I am Babu's sister and our mother is very ill."

Doctor asked her to tell him roughly what the family doctor had said. I would not know what exactly my sister told him but he asked her to go home straight away and stay with her mother. He would come within twenty minutes and no one should worry. My sister was probably sobbing when he came with another doctor, who looked very important. They conferred for a while and the other doctor gave my mother an injection. Our Doctor said that she would sleep calmly and an ambulance would come next morning to take her to the hospital. Doctor had a word with my father and consoled him a little. He must have guessed our father's nature and turned to my sister and instructed her what to do with the clothes, etc. All was taken care of from that point onwards.

I was away from the college at the time my mother became ill, on an educational visit to a construction site. It would have been difficult to find me, as long distance telephone calls were not readily available in those days. My sister wrote to me later about my mother's illness, after she had nearly recovered. Doctor told my sister that he would do everything as if he were part of the family. He asked her to trust him just as she would have trusted me. He also told her to leave me to my studies, knowing how keen I was and how demanding the first year in engineering was, compared with the science college years. He assured her that there was no point in worrying me unnecessarily, in any case. I could not be of any help and there would be no point in calling me back to Mumbai.

This must have been a torrid time for my sister. Doctor took care of my mother's stay at the hospital and the specialist treatment, but my sister had to arrange for my father's regular meals, her own work as a teacher and visit the hospital. Our relatives were not a great help. Some came to see my sister to offer consolation, assuming that my mother had been paralysed on one side of the body. Doctor had explained the problem to my sister well, which was apparently concerned with the condition of the nervous system and muscles. One old man came when Doctor was there. He did not know about the Doctor and started his roller-coaster diatribe about the medical profession. My sister told me later how Doctor had lost his temper and told him to stay away from the family. We lost a so-called relative but it did us some good, as the old man must have spread the news about the realistic condition of our mother!

My mother returned home from the hospital after some fourteen days. I went home for the end of term break and was overwhelmed to see her in her condition. She was already small and rather frail. With the illness, she had become a skeleton. Doctor had warned us not to be complacent and look out for any relapse or after effects of the treatment.

As if God was testing us, something worse followed soon afterwards. My mother started getting a rash on her left arm and the symptoms became more and more pronounced. The neighbours thought it was some contagious skin disease, which she might have got from another hospital patient, and some suspected that it could well be leprosy. They started keeping away from us. I could not blame them as there were phenomenal misconceptions about any contagious skin decease, for example, it could be hereditary and something to do with our past sins in this life or the previous ones, etc. Doctor gave us the strength and assured us that this was probably the reaction of the earlier treatment and our mother's skin had become too sensitive. He gave ointments and other medicines, as well as suggesting visits to a natural spring where the water had medical properties. It was impossible to get there by public transport. Fortunately, one of the workmen in my father's textile mill had started a business as a taxi-driver. His name was Resham Singh, a Sikh by religion, the same as many other taxi-drivers in Mumbai. We had known him as a boy and he spoke good Marathi. I went to see him and talked to him about our predicament. I explained to him what Doctor had told us and I tried to reassure him that my mother had no contagious disease of any sort. His words still ring true in my ears,

"Babusaab, I shall take you and your mother in my taxi in any condition, at any time of the day or night and anywhere you ask me to go."

He used to come to our house late in the evening, to avoid any traffic, and the eyes of anyone in the neighbourhood. My sister and I used to wrap up my mother in a clean sheet and I used to carry her on my back as one would give a piggy-back to a child. She weighed so much less that this was no trouble at all. It seemed like an old Indian mythological story, which described a son carrying his mother in this way, but this was the only sensible way to carry her. At the bathing place, Resham Singh and I would sit outside, while my sister would help our mother. Resham and I got to know each other very well and he became one of the family. His friendship with the family has lasted through all these years.

Just like the blessings received by the devoted children in the mythological story, it was a miracle that we had our mother back, fully cured, hale and hearty. I went back to my college, only after extracting a promise from my mother that she would not work too hard and, more important, not fall ill while was away! It might seem strange but she did keep her promise.

I soon finished my first year but not without problems. We had workshop practice including carpentry and smithy. The course was a hard one, with sixteen subjects to cope with and requiring project work as well, which was a cultural change compared with my previous educational experience. Only sixteen percent of the students could pass the first year examination every year and progress to the second year at the first attempt. The amount of submissions, drawings and reports meant working late at nights and it sapped my energy rather excessively. I had to pass, since I could not contemplate failure and the financial burden that would place on my family.

My stubbornness kept me going but, towards the end of the year, I felt rather unwell. I went through the written examinations somehow but the workshop examination was the hardest test I have ever faced in my life. The smithy test was about making an iron peg with a circular shape at one end and a point at the other. This required bending a straight iron bar with red hot heat and shaping it to the required geometry. I managed somehow but, when the test was finished, my left elbow seized up. I could not sleep with the pain. Next day, it was time for the carpentry test. The Head of the Workshop Department did not agree to postpone my test by a few days. He was a hurly-burly man from the North-West Frontier province of India, who disliked the soft Southerners. He refused to believe that my arm really hurt and thought that I was feigning illness. I got up the next day feeling like a wounded soldier with one more battle to survive. Perhaps like John Wayne facing the villains with only one good hand fit for using his gun! I had difficulty in using the saw to cut the piece of wood. I could just about use the mallet with the right hand and grip the chisel in the fingers of my weakened left hand. I somehow finished the joinery exercise, returned to my room and collapsed. By now, both my hands had seized up! Like me, my room partner had finished all his examinations on the same day. He helped me to pack my bags and put me on the night-sleeper train to Mumbai. I must have been a nuisance to my fellow passengers, unable to sleep and groaning a little with pain. The only sensible thing I had done was to phone Doctor and tell him when I would be at the Bombay Central station.

Doctor came to receive me with one of his neighbours.

"What is the matter with you lot? I just have got your mother on her feet and now it is you!"

He said this to cheer me up. He took me home just to put my bags away and meet my mother. Then we went to a nursing home where I was to spend the next fortnight on my back. My arms were not damaged as such and with some physiotherapy and thorough rest, I was as good as new. I met a nurse called Kamala there, an extremely charming young lady. Kamala, her sister Rekha and brother Sameer were from Bhopal, from the same place as our Doctor. They were a nice family, Kamala being the prettier of the two sisters and the youngest of the family. Her brother was very fond of her.

I finished my studies and came back to Mumbai in 1960. I used to meet Sameer and Kamala during the holidays. Kamala means a lotus flower in Sanskrit and she was like that. A friend used to comment that she is literally like that, born in a muddy and marshy place. He obviously knew about their family in Bhopal! I adored her and always looked forward to meeting her at Doctor's place.

One day, I went to his place in the afternoon and met Bayji in the Kitchen. His home was on the first floor of an old building, in two lots of rooms separated by a small corridor. On climbing the stair case, one came to the lounge and a bedroom, where all other visitors would go. Further along the corridor, there were toilettes and bathroom and two other rooms used as a kitchen and a work room, where family friends like me would call in first. The idea was to meet Bayji first, who would invariably be there, have a word or two and then go to meet Doctor in the lounge. I must have come rather unexpectedly that day and Bayji wanted to talk more than she normally did. She had a hint of sadness about her, but it was not too unusual. I heard some Indian dance music coming from their lounge and wondered what was going on. In the meantime, a servant from the neighbours came to ask for something and gave a very cunning smile. I was a little perplexed. In a few minutes, I caught a glimpse of Kamala leaving Doctor's lounge in a hurry. Bayji was not sure if I saw anything, but she insisted that I should have another cup of tea. I understood. That day, I left without meeting Doctor!

I came to know about the shadowy side of his character, little by little as time went by. I was determined to ignore it or even chose to disbelieve the stories, partly because it was none of my business and partly because I valued his other qualities. If Bayji could put up with him, we should do the same. His affair with Kamala made me a little sad, not only because I had a soft spot for her but also for the family's sake. It was rumoured that her mother was not married and she lived with a man in Bhopal. No young man would marry Kamala or her sister, unless he had a similar background. Doctor had done her and her sister some favours. He had got Sameer his job. As long as he prayed for forty minutes every day, perhaps he felt that he could be forgiven for a little wayward behaviour.

Doctor was very successful as a medical practitioner. Many times, I used to go to his dispensary after meals for an hour or so. It was in an area where mill-workers lived, within about twenty minutes walk from our home. Such visits gave me some exercise. Occasionally, I accompanied him on his home-visits, which gave me a chance to meet various people, rich and poor.

I have been to some of the poorest households in the world with Doctor. We looked frightfully out of place when we arrived in Doctor's car. He was well known in most such localities. The first thing to do was to park the car, mostly in front of a shop where *paans* were sold, beetle-nut leaves coated with lime and other flavoured coating. The *paanwallah* would summon a boy to look after the car, the hub-caps in particular. Doctor often accepted reduced payment from the poor and, at times, treated such people on credit, which was often forgotten.

Such losses were compensated by the sumptuous fees he received at the households in places like the Malabar Hill. Among his rich patients, I noticed that there were mainly elderly men and women, who seemed to trust him implicitly. I have never heard him say anything that might be remotely considered as out of place, let alone cause an offence. With men, he was a psychiatrist and he made a very effective use of this natural gift, which he had perfected with practice. With women, he was a charmer. He never said anything that would make any patient feel that his or her illness was not serious, taking care to ensure that he did not cause any alarm at the same time. Men were often told to ease up with the work and not to worry so much about the business. Women were asked to rest more and, where appropriate, delegate some tasks in management of the household to their daughters or daughters-in-law. Most women were doting mothers or mothers-in-law but they invariably felt that the younger women were not quite ready for such responsibilities! The younger women would often be listening and they were grateful to Doctor for putting in a good word. This served as a good investment for the future, I thought! In most such places, he was not just a medical practitioner but also a friend of the family.

These households, large apartments or detached houses, were steeped with riches, not made by one generation but many. The sitting rooms were spotlessly clean, with sofas clad with white silk covers and even a large tiger-skin on the floor in some places. However, it was the people that glowed with good life and brightened the homes, perhaps more than the furniture, ornaments and the decoration!

These people had no reason to pretend or be less than generous to anyone. When Doctor introduced me as an engineer, they showed a genuine delight that I had come to their home. While Doctor attended the patient, I was often invited to see their worship rooms. Here the statues of Gods were of pure gold inlaid with diamonds. The walls and floor were in marble and the ceiling was decorated with artwork depicting scenes from religious stories. It was a small wonder, therefore, that the God should bless these devotees with prosperity, in consideration of all these luxuries provided by them!

During one such visit, I met a businessman called Manoj Mehta. Doctor was called up to visit his brother Gopal. Gopal was much older than Manoj. They ran a family construction firm together and people often thought that they were father and son. The brothers had their flats next door to each other in Malabar Hill, an exclusive part of the city known for being a stronghold of rich people. Gopal was a widower and Manoj was a married man, with a loving wife, Sarita, and their three year old son, Keshav. Sarita was pretty, well-educated and very well-spoken. She looked after Gopal as well, treating him with the same respect as she would treat her father-in-law or her own father.

Gopal asked me to come and visit them whenever I could. He used to like talking about structural issues and often complimented me for my easy style of answering his questions. He had no formal training as an engineer but he was a shrewd businessman. He disliked engineers who used unnecessarily technical language to impress him. Manoj tried to become a qualified engineer but gave up after the first year. He could not cope with the rigours of the first year, as I had experienced in my case.

I used to visit the Mehta's home mostly with Doctor and also on my own. I used to see Gopal first but we moved next door to see Sarita, since Gopal liked her tea better than his servant could make. He used the excuse that I deserved a better treatment and that he could not poison me with what his servant called tea! We would normally wait until Manoj returned, often at about 10.30 pm. It was remarkable that Keshav would not sleep until his father came home, in spite of Sarita's loving care or mild reprimands. The boy would wait for his father, run to the door to greet him and make him sit sown. Manoj had to play a record, quite often the same every night. Finally, the boy would fetch a matchbox for his father to light his cigarette and then he would go to his bedroom.

In spite of their loving families, Doctor and Manoj were predatory men always on the look-out for clandestine adventures. Doctor believed that his lengthy prayers kept him protected from any guilt or perhaps he did not consider womanising as a sin at all. Manoj was also a Jain and a vegetarian, but he was partial to drinking and smoking. He believed that I was clever only in the academic sense but, otherwise, a simpleton and almost a fool. All the stories in Hindu epics, Ramayana and Mahabharata, were fiction to him. Under the guise of his being of a different faith, he used to ridicule Geeta. I put up with him for the sake of Gopal and Sarita, although his remarks were often quite offensive.

When I lost my first job in India, Gopal hinted a few times that I could join him and Manoj. However, the thought of being Manoj's colleague did not appeal to me. Manoj was not my type of engineer. His site practices were corrupt, to say the least. He was not the only contractor to bribe the local authority inspectors and get away with sub-standard work but seeing someone operate from such close quarters was disgusting for me. He used to pay comparatively low wages to his supervisors. He maintained that it was pointless to pay them more because they would cheat him in any case. He alleged that most foremen used less cement in concrete and sold off bags of cement on black market to line their own pockets. On one occasion, I shuddered with the thought of the bad quality concrete that went in his works. It could have some thirty percent less cement, if three lots of ten percent went to bribe the local authority supervisor, to supplement the foreman's salary and to the concrete suppliers for recouping the bribe they gave to Manoj for winning the subcontract.

Doctor and Manoj seemed to have no rules or limits to their adventurous games. I learnt about the professional ethics and about relationship between a doctor and a patient. This was nowhere in sight. I knew a nice Catholic family, mother, two brothers and a sister, a nice young girl working as a company secretary. The mother was taken ill and Doctor treated her. Later on, I saw once by pure accident that Doctor had taken the girl to see a film. He promised the girl a better job with Manoj's firm and literally passed her on to his fellow womaniser. I came to know later that Kamala's circumstances were similar but it was her older sister who became Manoj's victim. I often wondered earlier about Manoj working all that late, until half past ten every evening. Later I realised that he was spending money most evenings and not actually earning any!

During the last year of my life in Mumbai, I spent more than usual of my time in the company of this dynamic duo. I was out of work, miserable and vulnerable. Manoj was probably not really sorry to see a clever fool suffering this way. I sat gambling with them one night, soon after I had received my last salary cheque. I was winning but Manoj kept putting I O U notes instead of cash on the table. When I started loosing, I lost an amount equivalent to almost all of my salary. In the end, Doctor examined Manoj's I O U notes against my cash and I returned home with just about the sum I had. Manoj never gave me the extra sum he had lost, which I considered most despicable. Gambling was a sin but cheating this way and not paying for your losses were much bigger sins.

I had started to drink and most unusually, I once went to see a courtesan's show with them. Men used to hold big currency notes while a woman was singing some erotic songs. A girl would come closer, take the money and caress the enthusiast, often in an obscene manner. The singer would sing the song recommended by the highest bidder. Manoj continuously pestered me to do the same but I was nearly sick with the music and the whole thing was quite distasteful for me. I began to wonder whether, through gambling, drinking and visits to such places, Manoj wanted to relieve me of the sum my employers had given me as compensation for the loss of my job.

My dedication to my profession probably saved me from sliding down this slope. I decided to go to London for work and escaped all the embarrassment I might have caused my mother. She had memories of her father and my father's family, and she could not bear it repeating in my case. I can understand why she was happy for me to go away!

In 1973, Doctor visited America and had a stop-over in London on his way back to Mumbai. His friends in the USA had given him a Euro-Rail ticket as a present. All through his two-day stay with us, he was pestering me to buy the shares of some company and an old cottage in the suburb of Mumbai. I declined, having become wiser during my stay in London. He tried with Anna too, but she made me proud of her by saying that I made such decisions first. Doctor gave me the sad news of Manoj's death. He was found dead in the compound of a temple in Gujarat. The matter was hushed up, as Doctor told me, with a suspicion that someone had strangled him as revenge. I felt genuinely sorry for Manoj!

Doctor wanted to visit Rome and Anna agreed generously to let him visit her mother. I tried to persuade her otherwise and I was proved to be right. He made a pass at Anna's sister Carla and asked her to accompany him to see Italy. Her husband, Elio, would have slapped Doctor straight away but Carla restrained him. I had to face some embarrassment and repair the dented image of Indian people, by telling Carla about Doctor's background. However, I remained convinced that he should have excluded my sister-in-law from his ambitions and tried his luck outside the family.

I met Doctor briefly during my visits to Mumbai. I met him for the last time in 1996. My mother had stopped seeing him after I left Mumbai and she did not keep in touch with him any longer. He was a pale shadow of his earlier self. His wife was by his side and she warned me about his wandering thoughts. He told me about his attempt to sue the American firm for the disaster in his native city of Bhopal. I had known about it already. I was disgusted to hear him talk as an intermediary, willing to charge some three percent of a huge sum of five billion dollars. None of this was true, of course. He again asked me if I was interested in buying some property. He was the sort of person who never gave up!

I shall probably never see Doctor again. Perhaps with the influence of Western culture, I fleetingly wondered if he had not helped my sister with some ulterior motive. I could not think of this in Mumbai, in spite of having seen Manoj's attention drawn towards my sister and his invitation to her alone for some functions. I assumed this to be brotherly love, like my sister being his sister too! I hope that I would never find out, now that he is dead and Doctor has apparently drifted into a sad mental state.

11
First steps out in the cold

My decision to go to England or London in autumn 1968 may seem to be a courageous one after so many years. However, at that time, many of my friends and ex-colleagues thought that I was out of my mind. Some of them knew about the conditions in the UK construction industry and they believed that it was not the right time to get a good job as a civil engineer in London. Chances for an outsider like me must have seemed very bleak indeed. All the same, everyone wanted to help in whichever way they could.

Some of my ex-colleagues, who had lived in the UK earlier, gave contact addresses, some gave me their left-over British money for my Indian Rupees and many gave advice, which was rather peculiar. They told me about the land-ladies, table manners, etc., which worried me a little. I would have to learn the correct use of the bath tub very quickly, without spilling a single drop of water on the carpet. In Mumbai, we did not have a bath tub. One of my friends advised me that I should have some extra towels and spread them around the tub, in addition to the one meant for drying myself. I knew how to use a knife and a fork, but I could not use them as precisely as another friend of mine believed to be right! The right choice of knives and forks for salad, fish, meat, etc., seemed rather complicated to me. I pictured a British land-lady as a perfect person in every way, perhaps like the actress Julie Andrews, and I could not bear the thought of displeasing anyone like that. In the end, I chose to forget about these things. Perhaps I might never have to rent a room with a British land-lady! My main concern was about finding a place to go somewhere in London after arriving at the airport. I believed that the rest could then take its own course.

My hopes were pinned on meeting my childhood friend, Vijay, who had settled in London in 1962. Vijay and I had studied together at the same high school. He was the head-boy in our class, a bright and cheerful fellow, good at public speaking and an excellent cricketer. He was the Prime

Minister of our school parliament. Unfortunately, he had been a victim of the rules for admission to engineering and technical courses prevalent at that time. These rules depended on the result of an examination called "Intermediate Science". Aspiring students chose the science course after school and took this examination after two years of university study. We had to score well in science subjects (physics, chemistry and mathematics) but it was obligatory to get some minimum marks in language tests. It was ironic that Vijay, with all his skills as a public speaker, should fail the written test in Marathi, our mother-tongue! Everyone thought that it was a joke, until they knew the facts for certain. As a result, Vijay did a private course in automobile engineering and went abroad in 1962 for further training and work, while the rest of us got stuck in with our higher education and careers in Mumbai. I lost touch with him after the year 1965 but I somehow obtained his address in London and wrote to him about my plans to come to London in search of work. I asked him if it would be possible for him to meet me at the airport and help me initially, but he did not respond. In my mind, I felt sure that, if he had received my letter, he would help me.

If Vijay could come to the airport, many problems would be solved. As becomes an engineer, I had contingency plans, a decision tree for taking actions depending on the development of situation in stages. If Vijay was unable to come, I would make some phone-calls or go to an old lady called Mrs Banarase, who was reputed for providing accommodation for any stranded Mumbaiwallah at any time of the day! She was popularly known as *Ajibai* (Grandmother), so godlike, kind, selfless and generous that an Indian Pope would have made her a Saint! I kept this as the very last option, as I would be quite distressed to be forced to receive shelter in this way. My Kshatriya or warrior race ancestors would never have approved such a thing!

I boarded the Air-India plane on 17 November 1968, with some warm clothes, a list of addresses and some fifteen pounds in cash. My heart was heavy but my curiosity and sense of adventure kept me going. All through the nine or ten hours of the journey, I prayed with all my belief in the God that Vijay should come to meet me at the airport. The immigration control was not too bad and my luggage was retrieved without any problem. I walked with my trolley slowly, as if I was led by my destiny into the unknown, through a dark and unfamiliar passage.

My joy had no bounds when I saw Vijay at the exit, like someone holding a light at the end of a tunnel! We shook hands and he apologised for not responding to my letter in time. He had changed his residence and I did not know his new address. My letter had reached him after being redirected twice! In India, people would not move home unless there were exceptional circumstances. In London, it seemed commonplace among young people. My respect for the Royal Mail grew immensely, as such a thing about redirecting mail was quite new to me.

We took a taxi to Vijay's flat in Earls Court. We had so much to talk that we stayed up until early hours. Vijay shared the flat with Ben, an Indian of Jewish origin and an artist. They had no problem with my staying there until I got a job. Thereafter, I could either share the rent or move. Ben had a girlfriend, Mandy, who visited the flat for evening meals. Vijay and Ben had their rooms and I would have to camp in the sitting room. This was probably the best option available to me and I could certainly live with it for a month or two.

Ben saw that I had about fifteen pounds with me and helped me to buy a jacket and a pair of trousers suitable for formal occasions, like an interview for example. He also advised me to open a Post Office account with the remaining money. To enable me to meet my living expenses before getting any work, he told me that I should visit the local Social Security Office and get the unemployment benefit. He explained that this was not a charity but a form of loan. I would get work soon and pay income-tax to Her Majesty's

Ben

Government and, in this way, my loan would be repaid. Ben had a real gift for convincing people! I was already a chartered engineer and my dole money was fixed at some £7.50 per week. I paid £2.10 as my share of the rent, a third of the six guinea rent for the flat. About £2.00 went towards common shopping, which included weekly supply of milk, eggs, bread, onions and potatoes. If anyone was hard up and cash ran out towards the end of the week, which did happen occasionally with Ben, these common items of food came very handy.

I had lived away from home for my engineering studies, long enough to know how to survive without food cooked by someone at home. I was not a vegetarian like some other Indians I knew. I did not have any difficulties they had in changing their diet and food habits, to ensure intake of extra proteins essential suit the climate, much colder than they had ever experienced. I liked green vegetables, although I preferred them fresh. Here I had to make do with frozen spinach and beans. I could not eat beef but fish was fine with me, although potato chips were not the ideal substitute for rice. I soon found out the shops that used good cooking medium and developed a taste for fish and chips. Ben and Vijay gave me some lessons in basic cooking and I was soon able to cook well enough for myself. My mother did not believe me when I wrote to her since, in Mumbai, she would not allow me in the kitchen at any time!

Ben was the oldest and Vijay and I agreed with him on most things, including the shopping list. Within a week, I was financially independent, although with my head just above water. I had enough money for basic food, drink and going around on my own. Ben knew most things about London and he was my first mentor in so many ways!

I had some addresses of Indians given to me when I left Mumbai and I tried to contact them. Some Indian families were kind and treated me well but there were some, who were less than generous. One family from Goa was most discouraging and not welcoming. I got the feeling that they had set themselves up as Portuguese and did not want to renew contacts with anyone from India, unless they were as pale-skinned as themselves. Some Marathi people gave me the impression that all new immigrants, who came after they did, were responsible for the worsening of race relations in London! Some West Indian Asians were abusive of their ancestors to the extent that made me very uneasy. On the other hand, most Indians would readily complain about the way the indigenous people treated them but, in their turn, they would be very unkind in their opinions about the West Indians and Africans.

One day, I went to see an Indian family by appointment. It was a well-to-do family, husband and wife living together with three sons, who had finished their education and were working. I sat with them in their front room for a while, engaged in some polite conversation over a glass of orange juice. I soon realised that they were going away in turn to the kitchen. It dawned on me that they had their meals this way! I had already eaten beforehand but perhaps they did not want to risk asking me, in case I had not. One Brahmin gentleman would not tell me his profession but an acquaintance told me later that he was a bricklayer and handyman. His wife's sister was at the university and he was very proud of her. He told me so, almost to belittle me, I thought, and nearly suggested that he did not recognise my Indian Degree as anywhere as good as the UK degrees. He offered me a room to stay under very strict conditions, for example, I should help his wife as if she were my sister. He helped me to decide that I must stay on my own, away from such families, and choose company of fellow Indians very carefully.

Generally, I found the Indian housewives rather desolate, if not like fish out of water. They seemed to dislike the weather, the absence of social life as they knew it and the cold behaviour of their British counterparts. They thought that they had made a great sacrifice in coming to London, leaving behind the luxuries of their parents' homes, servants, etc. They would seek to keep within a certain circle and not mix with any other women. I am happy to see that the second generation of Asian girls have a different attitude. However, the housewives at that time convinced me that it must be an awful idea to go to India and return with a wife, who did not know all the facts about life in the West. In my case, I could see myself becoming a confirmed bachelor. I might soon ask myself, "Why should I get married?", if not "Who will marry me?", having passed the early twenties and the stage when one would worry about the question "When shall I get married?".

My search for work started with Ben lending me his typewriter and Mandy helping me with the first draft of an application for work. I wrote some sixty applications within a week. I had never used a typewriter earlier but I did manage to learn the hard way and on my own. I was concerned that my letters had to be good enough for the purpose. All I could do was to hope for the best! My prayers were answered and, within two weeks, I received four calls for interview. I had some idea about the work I should start with and the salary I should get. Accordingly, I had decided to wait and choose properly, so that I could have a good start in my new career.

Two offers were not worth any thought but the other two seemed good. However, one position was not available until the middle of December. The other firm was owned by a sixty year old engineer of Polish origin, an ex-RAF captain who had served in Calcutta during the Second World War.

My interview with this gentleman was remarkable in so many ways. He was smartly dressed and sported a military-style moustache with pointed ends under his sharp nose. He might have been similar to Mr Bailey, uncle Hari's benefactor, although I never saw Mr Bailey personally. He seemed to know about Indians, their proficiency in engineering and their general way of thinking, perhaps better than many Indians. He asked me a number of questions and showed interest in employing me straight away, without beating round the bush. I had no problems with knowledge in structural design and the British Codes of Practice. He was amused when I told him that the Indian Codes were adapted from the British Codes, occasionally with the same mistakes! I was pleased that I had prepared well and read the technical journals, as he seemed to be well-informed and aware of the industry issues, even though he was in such a senior position. He had also known about me a little from a senior Indian engineer. In the end, he pulled out a six inch long slide rule and did some sums for a minute or so. This was indeed a big surprise for me!

"You are a Chartered Engineer but without any experience in the UK, twenty-eight years old and unmarried. I could offer you £1,320 per year."

This offer seemed to be near the lower limit of my expectations but it was not too bad. I could have my turn to surprise him, I thought. I said that I would accept his offer for the first three months. He should then see me after three months and review my salary. He gave me one of his sharp looks but agreed and gave me another jolt.

"You haven't got much money left with you, have you?"

I said that I had some nine pounds.

"That is not enough. Go and ask Mr Powell to give you £75.00 advance. You are alone here, my boy, all on your own. You need more money in hand, enough for at least a month."

I could not believe my ears! This man was prepared to trust a stranger and a foreigner. He was prepared to give me a loan without any collateral. Such helping hand had suddenly elevated me from the position of an indigent Indian to a member of the British civil engineering profession and not just trebled my income of some £30.00 a month! I came to Vijay's flat on cloud nine. My next visit was to the Social Security Office to thank the officer and tell him about my change in circumstances. The second visit was to a wine shop. Ben, Vijay, Mandy and I were happy and drunk that evening!

As if by coincidence, I received an offer from the firm who had interviewed me earlier. This would have given me a salary some £200.00 higher than I had accepted. Ben and Vijay did not believe this and Ben told me to jump at it. But I could not do this. I could also not give Ben my reasons and convince him that I had given my word and, as a Kshatriya, I must abide by it.

I started work on 9 December. My employer called me again after three days.

"I hope that everything is all right with you, Desai."

He asked with a tone that was pretty genuine. I thanked him and said that I was making good progress and settling down with my work.

"I know. John (the section leader) seems quite happy with you. By the way, I give some bonus to the staff at Christmas for their year's work. But you will have worked with us for such a short time, less than a month."

I said that he had already helped me with the loan, which I appreciated very much. I thanked him and said that the bonus could wait until the following year, so that I would have really earned it. He seemed very pleased with my answer and said,

"Let us add a nominal £10.00 to your salary for December, shall we?"

I thanked him again and did not know, for once, what else to say!

Three months passed and I requested Mr Powell for a meeting with the Chief. He was shocked when I told him that I wished to have my salary reviewed. He said that this was unheard of but fixed an appointment for me, any way. He murmured about the Chief's formula for salaries, containing qualifications, age, marital status, degree, etc. Rumour had it that the scale had the Ox-bridge Englishmen at the top, sliding down in a descending order for other Englishmen, Scots, Welshmen, West Europeans, East Europeans and Asians! For Asians, there was a maximum limit and so on so forth. I did not believe this and went to see the Chief in his Office.

I reminded him politely about our agreement and said that I wished to have my salary reviewed. He seemed surprised although not genuinely in his mind, I thought. He must have asked my section leader and he seemed well informed. He asked me about my expectations. I did not tell him about the other offer, but asked for a sum of that order. Out came the slide-rule and we paused for two minutes.

"I can't pay you that salary."

He said this like a good poker player, stroked his moustache gently and stared at me. We paused again for half a minute. I knew from others that he did this and said this sentence only when he could agree with you! It sounds strange but, if he were not to touch his moustache and say anything else, I would have known that I had a problem.

"But, I could pay you an extra bonus, which will give you more or less the same amount!"

We agreed. Mr Powell expressed his surprise as I expected him to do, being a true-blood accountant concerned about the salary-bill and finances of the firm. He wondered what the other newly employed Indian engineers would feel, if they knew about my salary. Perhaps he was mistaken about the Chief's sliding salary scale! I knew that the Chief paid some senior Indian engineers well and according to their abilities. It is possible, however, that some junior and new Indians may have behaved in a spineless manner and allowed Mr Powell to treat them unfairly. Some expected to be treated badly or with discrimination, perhaps they did not believe in themselves or they needed some excuses to hide their inadequacies and lack of initiative. They gave an impression that all Indians could be without self-respect and Mr Powell was perhaps shocked to have a different experience with me.

While I was well-equipped as far as the work went, I was woefully backward and ill-informed about many aspects of my new world. First, I was amazed with the freedom the girls had and that they could go around alone so late in the evening. Pre-marital sex was not quite a taboo for me but I was not in a rush and I was prepared to wait for the right time to come! In the meantime, Mandy, Ben's girl friend, became a good friend. I could talk to her freely and she even introduced me to other girls. However, I was very shy and, as Mandy said, perhaps too polite with them. They expected to go out for a drink and a meal and have fun. Under such circumstances, another young man might have started a relationship with one of Mandy's friends but I believed in a longer game than the girls did! Perhaps as Sulu used to say, I thought too much about so many things!

During the first few days, one of the simple things to puzzle me was the bravery of girls walking in the cold weather, with their legs exposed. One evening, I asked Mandy about it and she rolled over laughing. She clasped my hand, put it on her thigh and exclaimed,

"We wear transparent stockings, you silly Indian boy!"

I must have blushed so much that Ben gave me a look of a jealous husband. Later on during my stay, Mandy added to his discomfiture by telling him that I spoke English better than him. Ben liked to pose like a Jew from Iraq and spoke with a distinct lisp. Mandy told him that he should not hide his Indian origin and be honest like me. Strangely enough, Mandy seemed very keen to know about my exploits at work as the days went by. She seemed to grow fond of me and often wanted to know about my life in India. I began to feel a little uneasy, perhaps owing to my sense of gratitude to Ben. After some six months, I felt that I could not go on like this and it was time to leave that place. I soon found a suitable bed-sitter in Notting-Hill-Gate and moved. I kept in touch with Vijay and met him before he returned to India for good in 1971. He told me that Ben had gone to Israel for work and that Mandy could not go with him. She had married a divorced man with children, working with the Embassy in Chile, and had left London.

Apart from work, I had two other interests, table-tennis and German language. I was a member of YMCA and played for their team in the Central English League for one season. I often had a game of table-tennis, followed by shower, and came to the Underground station on my way to the room. If I had time, I used to stop at a very friendly Irish Pub nearby for a Guinness. I came to know some Irish people, regulars at the pub and a very jovial type. One young man once asked me why an Indian like me would like an Irish drink like Guinness.

"It is quite simple really."

I replied with a straight face.

"The glass of Guinness could look like an Indian just like me! Dark and with a good head on it!"

I still remember the ripple of good-natured Irish laughter all round the pub!

I soon came to know about the Linguist Club in Kensington, where I could do both things, table-tennis and German conversation. It was a vibrant place, with Europeans, South Americans and African members. Social life was wild at times, with frequent parties and dinner-dances. I learned dancing a little, although such skill was not really called for, because the dance floor was very small and the music loud and modern. The club had a few Asian-looking members but no-one would admit to have an Indian language as their mother-tongue or belong to India or Pakistan. They were either from Africa or from Singapore or some part of the world other than the Indian subcontinent! Also, no one had come to find work, like I did. Most of them had come to become aerospace engineers or computer scientists. I believed them all but the other Europeans wondered how I was the only pure Indian around! It was rumoured that the lady members were not impressed with men of Indian origin. I did not care for such falsehood.

I soon formed friendship with a German called Manfred and two Englishmen, Paul and Tony. Paul lived in Chiswick, where he had a business as an estate agent. He found a better flatlet for me in Turnham Green area. This was very convenient for us, as Paul, Tony and I could play as a team in the local table-tennis league. The three of us were table-tennis people but Manfred was the ultimate group-leaderI ever came across. People laugh when I tell them now that I was among the few people that were once thrown out at 3.00 am from a house where Manfred had his party. At such parties, I would normally be one of the organisers as Manfred appreciated my skills in organising these parties. He made me believe that Germans were the best when it came to enjoying weekends and parties, after a hard week's work.

Manfred's entourage had some core members like me but he seemed to have some very agreeable newcomers from time to time. I always wondered about his charismatic gift for choosing people. I believed this to be a natural and God-given talent. Girls liked him and trusted him. He told his friends that he had a childhood sweetheart and, one day, he would go to Bonn and marry her. There were no questions of emotional ties or entanglements and everyone knew where they stood with him.

One day in March 1970, a married Italian woman joined our group, Angela by name, thirty-two years of age, very charming and intelligent. She was really proficient in German and Spanish. Oddly enough, she was also a graduate in Mathematics. On a number of occasions, we found each other in the kitchen doing the washing-up and sharing jokes on other party people. She told me about her married life in Turin, her husband's devotion to his career with the FIAT car company and her four year old son Davide. Davide was with his Nonna (grandmother) and Angela missed him very much. She had won a scholarship to come to England for one year to do an advance course in computer programming.

I admired Angela's academic excellence but it was her attitude to life that amazed me. She was the first young lady, with whom I could joke freely and speak privately on any sensitive subject without any fear of embarrassment. She was apparently shocked when she knew that I was a celibate at the age of thirty. She did not show her surprise openly or say anything that would have hurt me. In her inimitable manner, she said a few times that something must be done about it and tried to fix me up with a girl

Angela

she knew. It did not work, just as it had not worked when Mandy had tried to arrange dates for me. I simply could not be intimate with a girl without knowing her well enough as a person. Little did I know that my wishes were to come true on one unforgettable evening, when something happened that was to change my life.

Some club members, like me, did not have their own cars and public transport was not convenient late at night after the club events. Most of the times, Manfred used to take some of us home in his Volkswagen Beetle. My room was not far from Angela's and we were usually the last to be dropped off. On one such occasion, I was in a great mood, after a hard day's work and a long enjoyable evening at the club. I asked Angela to come to my room for coffee, as I had often done before. She chided me as usual for making advances to a married woman and called me a "cheeky Indian boy". But this time she came and we had coffee and cognac. She never called me an Indian boy again, after she left me next morning as a man.

All my past had evaporated in the warmth of this marvellous angel. I had bridged the gap between the East and West, as far as my prescriptive ideas in family values were concerned. I still remember the following few months as "those were the days" in my life, when I came of age for the second time. Angela used to spend evenings with me, cook for me and love me in a manner I was to rediscover later in my life when I met my future wife.

Our farewell was painful but it took place with propriety. She had to go back to her son Davide and I understood her. She told me that I must get married and to a nice girl, which would certainly come along one day. When I told her about the probability of my remaining a confirmed bachelor, she laughed. She knew enough about me to be convinced that I was not cut out to remain a bachelor. Such people were different and she could tell from her experience. I did not delve into this matter too much but I did not indulge in a film dialogue either, to say that no other girl could be as nice to me as she was! In the long term, she belonged somewhere else for sure. Like the angels that come to earth for a short time, she came in my life for a while, only to change it for the better, irrevocably.

My friend Manfred left London after some six months and went back to marry his childhood sweetheart in Bonn. His fare-well party was an event to remember. I had a Swedish lady-friend by that time, Sophie by name, who was an extra-ordinary cook. She often argued with Martin, the Linguist Club cook from Portugal and a friend of mine. He often told her that he put up with her for my sake and Manfred's sake, but I think he quite liked her in his own Latin way! They put on a party for Manfred, which was a culinary delight and a battle between the two grand-champions in the art of cookery, from the North of Europe and from the South.

Early in the morning, Manfred thrust the keys of his car in my hands and said,

"Babu, this is my parting gift to you! Let Sophie take you home because I can't do it today. Goodbye and have a good life!"

I could not take it for free and handed him some two hundred pounds, which was all I had! I soon got my licence, thanks to Sophie and my good fortune in not having any accident during the bizarre training sessions. Her excellence in cooking must have left no room for any other orderly thoughts in her mind. She insisted on laying the table tidily but she was thoroughly messy otherwise. She was a wild type and often wanted to go to night-clubs with other girls, some friends and me. I had recently acquired a credit card and it seemed convenient to pay without worrying at that time. She was not dishonest by nature but naturally exuberant. She seemed to have sufficient money to buy expensive dresses for herself and she would turn up sometimes with expensive gifts for me. I could not say no to her in any event. I was drawn into a whirlwind lifestyle, as if the pendulum had swung to the other extreme away from my way of life in Mumbai.

I knew that my work was getting more and more demanding, as I was given a senior position. The firm was tolerant in many ways and time-keeping was not a problem for professional staff. Nevertheless, I became known for my "whispering phone-calls" to say that I would be late after a night out with Sophie. Strangely enough, one of the partners thought better of me for this. He was known to be a regular late night frequenter of pubs and places of entertainment and he was glad that he had an Indian convert into his way of life!

It was quite unexpected when the time for Sophie's departure came. We had a party and Martin was at his best. For once, he succeeded in cooking on his own! I cannot describe how the evening became midnight and the dawn followed, when Sophie picked up her bags to go to Heathrow directly from Turnham Green. Paul took us there and she went, in the same cheerful manner as she had been all through the farewell party.

I remember the way I came back to my little flat with Paul and sank in an armchair. I felt like a battered ship coming to the harbour after a long journey through storms and rough seas. I did not know where I stood, I was emotionally drained and financially broke. Life seemed quite empty all of a sudden. I had a strong urge to go back to Mumbai and forget I ever came to London. I am not sure what would have happened if Paul were not there with me.

We had some coffee and he started talking about the local table-tennis league, the new season and how we could win the league division during the winter and gain promotion if we prepared well. I was half-listening in the beginning but Paul knew that I had to come back to normal, one way or the other. He told me that perhaps I should change my job and get paid better. He saw to it that I would dress up and go to work, although a little late in the day.

A few weeks later, Paul invited me to a party with his Italian girl-friend Claudia. Claudia was pretty, small but very lively. I had met her beforehand and I liked her very much. I had been to some parties after Sophie's departure but sat out in a corner most of the time, nursing a beer as long as I could. That evening, I got ready to go with Paul and Claudia and waited for them in my flat. However, he came alone and with a worried look on his face. Claudia was ill. We decided to go and see her.

Claudia's bed-sitter was a mess and one of her friends, Anna, was tidying it up. We had seen this girl at the club before but she would go straight home after the conversation classes and stopped in the cafe for some food only and a brief chat with Claudia and other girls. No one would make an effort to invite her to any party because she had probably declined once. Here she was, however, cleaning Claudia's place as her big sister would do. She had come early in the afternoon, worrying how Claudia could go out that night in her condition. She had helped Claudia to clean up, tucked her up in her bed and given her some hot soup, hoping that she might get better in time to go to the party. In the end, Claudia did not improve much and Anna had to phone Paul to tell him so.

Within a few minutes of seeing us, Claudia seemed to have miraculously perked up. Perhaps the hot soup had done its job or perhaps it was not in her nature to be miserable in the company of friends. After a while she said,

"Look, Paul, I should rest now but why don't you take Anna home? She has already done a lot and she should rest now as well. I shall be as good as new tomorrow morning."

We left and I remembered that I had not eaten anything except for a sandwich after breakfast. Paul was in the same state and I asked him if we should go to an Indian restaurant. Anna asked Paul if we could drop her at the tube station. I insisted that we could do no such thing and that she should come with us. I have not seen an expression on a girl's face like I saw on Anna's at that moment. It was partly disbelief, partly gratitude and perhaps some relief. She looked really tired and hungry, I thought. She looked at Paul and he also insisted that she had to come with us, with all his courtesy and charm as an officer and gentleman.

It was one of the most enjoyable meals. Paul was a charmer and superb conversationalist. He knew what the Italians liked to talk about and made Anna very comfortable and at ease. I had never heard her talk so much but, this time, her words were flowing like a stream with the blocking obstacle removed. She knew enough about Indian food as, naturally, she had eaten out often enough in the company of her colleagues. We must have finished pretty late at night and Paul took Anna to her room. Before we departed, he made her promise that she would come with Claudia for the next party.

After this event, the four of us almost became inseparable. I had a strange feeling whether Paul had the same effect on Anna, as Sulu had on me when I was five years old! She was a changed person and she amazed many members of the club with her transformation. She came to be known for her skills for arranging parties and outings. She would do so if Paul, Claudia and I could go. She was most discreet about everything she did as an ideal hostess and people simply loved her for this.

At Christmas time, Claudia invited us to her home town near Rome. I found it odd but we agreed to meet there, while Paul and I would stay in Rome, where Anna's family lived. Anna insisted that we stay in her sister's flat which would be empty, as she would be at her in-laws over Christmas. It was all arranged with Anna's precision as usual.

Anna's mother was as near a perfect *mamma* as one could ever hope for. She took an instant liking for me and, like any Indian lady I had known before, seemed to believe that I always needed something more to eat and drink. She wanted to say a lot to us, but I had to depend on Anna's translation. One of the things she said was that she wished Anna's father were alive and I could meet him. Anna's brother was not so friendly to start with but he seemed to be impressed to know that I was an engineer. He spoke a little English and made me promise that next time I would have learnt enough Italian to understand his Mamma. That was enough, he suggested as an aside, because she would do the talking most of the time, any way!

That is exactly what I had to do before going to Rome next time. Soon after Christmas, we had decided that she should share the flat with me, so that I could learn Italian quicker, as she had the patience to teach me.

It might seem strange but there were similarities in the background of my family and Anna's. Her mother was brought up nearly as an orphan, like my father, and she seemed to value hard work as much as a devotion to the God, as the life had taught her right from her childhood. She was pleasantly liberal in her religious views. She had read about some Indian saints and understood the logic behind pantheism. She was against any commercial and religious establishment. She disliked the Christian Democratic Party for the alleged corruption and association with the Mafia. This was probably because she was devoted to Anna's father, a Protestant and an Anglophile, who had worked hard during the war to help Jews and was helped by some Jewish businessmen later in his life. On the minus side, his sister had come to live with them and Anna's mother had suffered looking after her, although not as badly as my mother had suffered soon after her marriage, on account of my old vagabond of a grandfather. Anna's old aunt had some money, but a large part of it was allegedly taken away by the local priest for the Church, with promises made to the old lady before she died, of eternal happiness in heaven.

In addition to these similarities in our background, one event really showed up the common way of thinking shared by Anna and I. Once I was walking back home with Claudia, Anna and a Canadian intellectual, Dr Mann, who invited us to see his large caravan parked near our home. Dr Mann was a professor at a Canadian university and a very rich man, well past fifty years of age. He had divorced his wife, left a small island and home to her and wandered off to Europe in his large camper and cash, to travel and lead a free life. He was big and almost arrogant, except when he played table-tennis, which he did only moderately well. Claudia was somewhat fascinated by his clever talk. We had a couple of drinks and Dr Mann wanted us to watch some videos. I had to start early next day. Anna and I excused ourselves but Claudia said that she would stay a little longer. We walked away but we stopped suddenly after some hundred yards. Instinctively, we turned back and ran towards Dr Mann's caravan. I knocked on the door and Anna asked Claudia for keys to her room and said,

"I just remembered that I left my keys in your room. I couldn't get in my place without them."

Claudia said that she would come with us instead of staying any longer. I saw a look on Dr Mann's face, roughly like that of a wolf who had to let the little red-riding-hood get away! We came to Claudia's room for Anna to collect her keys. I suspect that she probably had them all the time and only pretended to have found them on Claudia's table! Anna's smile told me that we had felt the danger and knew what had to be done, simultaneously and without exchanging any words.

In May 1971, Anna and I got married. Angela was right! I was not the type who could remain a bachelor. I phoned my mother and she sounded quite happy, although she could not come to England herself. Others, including my sister, seemed unhappy but they would understand later on, I thought. Anna's mother was delighted.

In June 1971, we went to Rome. We met Anna's family properly, including her sisters, Carla and Sonia, and their families. I shall describe the Rome visit separately but, in the good old Indian tradition, I feel that I should first pay respect to the elder members of the family.

We went to Parma to see Anna's uncle Gino. My first meeting with Gino has been one of the most memorable events for me. He was the eldest brother with three sisters, who had to flee Argentina when their father had some disagreement with the dictatorial regime. The children were placed in various families. Gino was on his own at the age of fifteen. He started as a trainee electrician with the state railway at Parma and looked after his sisters. Anna's mother got married and moved to Rome and the other two married locally in Parma in due course.

During the post-war time, many blocks of flats were built in Parma and Gino had done the electrical work for a few. He was a well-known figure in his locality. When I first met him, he asked me if I wanted to see anything particular in Parma. He thought that I would probably want to see the Museum or the Cathedral. Instead, I asked him if I could visit the factories where they made Parmesan cheese and ham. He looked very impressed. After a few phone-calls, we were on our way for an experience in my life, which I remember for two different reasons.

First, I noticed with some mild concern that he drove his car rather badly for an Italian. Especially, he did not change the gears properly and drove in lower gears most of the times. I knew later from Anna that he drove his car only from the railway station to home. Until he was fifty-five, when he retired, he had never taken out a driving licence. He did not need any because everyone knew him well, including the police. He managed to get one after some struggle but old habits never left him!

The second reason for not forgetting that trip was the high regard all our hosts held for Gino. These people knew him not just as an electrician but as a father figure, who had helped many farmers during their difficult times. The factories were run by families, one or more as co-operatives, in a manner that showed their devotion for the work. They knew that the factories provided them and their families with a livelihood. They were clean and tidy, and maintained very professionally. In one factory, a lady was explaining the cheese-making process to us and a worker came to call her. She excused herself, took out the tool box and returned within ten minutes. She had corrected some fault herself! Not in England, let alone in India, had I seen such efficient and capable female factory owner.

Gino and I spent quite some time together. I got used to his accents and he was too great a man to mind my beginner's Italian. Finally, it was time to part. Gino was in tears.

"I was praying all the time that Anna should meet someone like you and get married!"

The grand old man said this with true feelings. My mother had blessed our marriage but Gino's words brought a lump in my throat. After all, I had met one of my people, well away from Mumbai, who meant so much to me, just like Dadaji and Mirzasaab!

I was often sad with the feeling that I was not fortunate enough to meet Anna's father. But Gino was like a father-in-law to me and no one could have done more for us than he did. He was so kind and generous with us every time we saw him and we kept in touch over the phone regularly, until he passed away in 1997.

Gino's wife, Antonella or Nella for short, was just as good to us as Gino was. They had one daughter also called Anna, a nurse, and a son. I inadvertently complimented Nella that their apartment was so tidy. She said with tears in her eyes,

"Babu, I wish one of my children would marry and I have a grandchild who will make everything untidy. I am tired of this tidiness, my son!"

On 28 December 72, Anna had our first daughter, a late Christmas present or an early new year gift! We named her Asha, a word for hope in Marathi. Anna's mother, Nella and Gino made such a fuss about her during our next visit that I cannot really describe. Gino's other sisters had grandchildren and Anna's sisters had children too. But Italian grandparents have unlimited love for the little ones and it grows with growing number of grandchildren! I was not so fortunate with my grandparents, but I knew what I would have missed, if I were to be born in Italy!

My mother was delighted with her first grandchild, so was Sulu and everyone else in Mumbai. Just like the quotation from "Alice in Wonderland", all seemed to have won and all seemed to have won prizes, in two different continents!

12
Elio

I often wondered why Anna was not born in Mumbai or a nearby place in India. This must have been a rare mistake of one of our Gods responsible for creating the life on earth. Perhaps He left our case to a lesser official, in the department responsible for forward planning of human marriages and births. Hindus believe that couples are made to be with each other not only for one life but also from one generation to the other. If one partner should die, his or her soul is kept in heaven until the other arrives. At an opportune time in the programme made by this department in

Elio

heaven, a pair is sent back to the earth with a gap of some three or four years to be born within a reasonable geographical distance of each other. In our case, the official was probably a trainee or perhaps he had one glass too many of some heavenly drink. It is conceivable that he was under the influence of an angel serving the drink and he kept thinking about her sweet smile well into the next day at work. He must have packed up the female life-form of my other half, some five years after my birth in Mumbai, and sent it to earth at a location missing its destination by some four thousand miles! To be fair to the heavenly system, the package may have been sent correctly but it may have collided with a meteor on its way and got deflected from its intended path.

It appears that, although we grew up well apart, we had some similarities in our character, which must have been carried by our souls from generation to generation. The heavenly powers must have arranged to bring us together in London, as there is no better meeting place in the world for lost souls! Finally, we got married as the God had intended.

One of the first questions we had to tackle was about our families. Soon after we had decided to renew our eternal partnership in life, Anna asked me if we should visit Mumbai, so that she could meet my family or go to Rome so that I could see everyone from her family, including her sisters and uncle Gino. As a fine upstanding Indian, I was most willing to give Anna the first choice. We decided to go to India, since I had seen her mother and her brother already although not her sister and the rest of her family. However, it was the month of June. Mumbai weather becomes stifling hot before the rain starts and very humid in early days of the rainy season. We say that we should not invite even our enemies to Mumbai in June. How could I subject my wife to these tortures? It was most certainly not the right time of the year for a visit to Mumbai. Besides, we had to have inoculation, Anna's visa, money for fares, presents, light-weight clothes, etc.

On balance, it seemed easier and less expensive to go to Rome. We were still in our honey-moon mode and neither of us was ready for a serious argument. Anna also understood my point that I should brief her fully about the characters in Mumbai before we went there. While I had met some of Anna's family, my power of expression was not good enough to create passable and quick pen-pictures of Mumbai people for Anna. I was also worried about the tolerance of Indian female folk, other than my mother, towards a woman from another continent. I could not rely totally on Anna's understanding and good nature, since I feared that she may have some difficulty to start with in Mumbai, knowing our women as well as I did.

We finally landed at Rome. I was looking forward to the Roman experience more fully this time, with an added benefit of my fledgling-like knowledge of Italian language. Just as we came out of the customs into the arrival area, a six-foot tall man with dishevelled and thinning hair approached us with speed. Before I knew what was happening, he kissed Anna on both cheeks and turned to me. As if in self-defence, I took a couple of quick steps backwards and extended my hand. Anna recovered in the meantime and exclaimed,

"This is Elio! My sister Carla's husband."

Elio clasped my hand with his strong grip and shook it until the elbow joint began to rattle. He was simultaneously laughing and talking rapidly. I got to know him well during this first encounter. He could not care if I did not understand him but it was important that he had to talk. I understood a little, some translation by Anna helped and I got the gist of his exuberant welcome. He seemed to have formed a good opinion about me. He was sharp enough to understand my concept of expressing friendship with men and my limits of affection between male relatives. It was clear to him that I would go only as far as shaking hands and not kissing on cheeks.

When we reached home, I was introduced to Elio's sons, Carlo and Paolo. Carlo, the older brother, was five years of age and Paolo was three years old. They were both handsome, tidy and courteous. For quite some time, they looked puzzled and disappointed. I asked Anna to find out if there was anything the matter. So she did and everyone laughed. The boys expected me to be wearing war paint and feathers in the head! They knew what "Indians" looked like from what they had seen in the Western films. I could understand their feelings when they saw that I was not a red-skin and, with the exception of my complexion being on the darker side, I was not vastly different to anybody they had known.

Carla, the eldest of the three sisters, met Elio at the time of Rome Olympics. Carla was a volunteer in the section looking after female athletes and Elio was a referee and an official for the boxing competitions. He was among the young Italian males out for conquest in the large gathering of talented girls from all over the world and with beautiful bodies. Even before that event, Elio was renowned for his prowess as a womaniser and no one thought that he would ever get serious with a girl. Carla had all the attributes he admired but she was a far more serious and intelligent girl, than those in Elio's world. From what Anna told me, I gathered that Carla gave him the brush-off when they first met. His male ego was probably hurt too much to come to terms with this. His chauvinistic and strong man tactics got him nowhere. But he had made up his mind that Carla was the girl for him and he persisted. Within a few days, Elio was hurt badly as he got caught in some skirmish between rival gangs supporting two boxing teams. Carla must have felt sorry for him and went to visit him in the hospital a few times. After recovering from his broken arm, Elio was encouraged by Carla's visits to the hospital. He could wait no longer and called at Carla's house one Sunday morning, quite unexpectedly, when Carla was not at home. He met her father, told him that he wanted to marry Carla and that he could not live without her. He said that he would commit suicide if he was rejected by the family and fainted on the spot! Carla's father did not know what had descended on the family! He somehow saw the young man off. When Carla came home later, her father asked her for an explanation. Carla knew Elio too well to know that he meant what he said. She perhaps had developed a soft spot for him during the time he was in the hospital. Perhaps she belonged to that group of females who believed that they had a mission to help and build up the life of undeserving and delinquent young men! In the end, they got married.

Carla had her career and the two boys. She had her Mamma to take care of them but she needed her own family as well. She put up with Elio and developed her own way of dealing with him. She earned a good salary, much more than he did as a low grade government employee. He did not care much for promotion, which needed a certain qualification. Carla and her brother tried very hard but to no avail. On the other hand, he could cook and do some good proportion of the house-work. He used to compliment me on my education, my courage in settling down in a foreign country, etc. I told him in return that my achievements were as effective as the hundred strokes of a goldsmith. They could not match his single hit like an iron-smith, marrying a clever girl like Carla. I was confident that Anna would not take an offence when I said this!

I have really listed as many plus points about Elio as one could ever do. Elio had one of the rare distinctions of being universally unpopular. Carla's sister, Sonia, and her husband hated him most. He had tried to cast aspersions on all eligible females in the family, at one time or the other. With Sonia, he was particularly unpleasant.

Sonia was very different to both Carla and Anna. I used to say that Carla was the cleverest, Sonia was the prettiest and Anna was the happy medium. They all took it in the right spirit. Sonia wanted to become a teacher but she did not get through the qualifying examination in Rome. She would have got admission in other cities. However, her mother was not very keen and Sonia was very much attached to her from her childhood. According to their mother, she was of a nervous disposition and couldn't have managed it on her own in another city. I think she would have made a marvellous teacher. When I told her about my mother and the way her life was taken over by the students in the neighbourhood, she was really moved. Even with my modest Italian, I used to tell her stories about my school life and about the kind teacher who helped me initially. Elio was very sour about our good relations with Sonia. He almost gave a clear hint that we should be on his side and, hence, not be so cordial with Sonia and her husband.

I have admired Sonia's husband, Luigi, for his painting and small sculptures. We have a few of them still with us. He was discarded by his mother and a local orphanage had taken him in. He tried to find his mother but the rules of the orphanage would not let him. Elio always passed very unkind remarks about Luigi's background. Luigi was athletic and he had played football for the local team in his youth. He was handsome and an excellent match for Sonia. They met when Sonia was working in a nursery school. He was working in a factory that made cakes. They got engaged but Sonia's parents were not in favour of Luigi. Not only because he was an orphan, but they also did not like the fact that he had no education and he was only a manual worker. Nevertheless they decided to get married. Sonia got a job in Luigi's firm and their romance flourished. The date for the marriage was fixed, the church ceremony was arranged, all of Luigi's football friends got ready for the big event. Being a member of the staff and a popular one, the cake manufacturer baked a magnificent wedding cake.

The marriage was to take place in the evening but the lady luck had written a different script for the lovers. Sonia's father had a heart attack in the morning. Elio promptly went to the church to cancel the wedding but the authorities would not let him, unless Luigi's friend, who had made the arrangements, told them so. How could the wedding go ahead when the girl's father was ill? Anna's father recovered and the first thing he said was to let the marriage go ahead. He loved Sonia as much as he loved the other children and her big day was not to be spoilt. Luigi went to see Anna's father and said that they would not go ahead unless he felt better. It was obvious that the old man was not going to be well enough to give away his daughter but he insisted that the marriage must not be postponed. He was superstitious and, according to his belief, it would be a very bad thing to postpone something that was agreed with the priest. It could sound strange but, in India, some orthodox people believe in exactly the same thing, although it is related to the precise time agreed with priest and based on the position of planets at the time of the birth of the bride and the groom. The marriage went ahead although as a low key affair. Elio spread rumours about the heartlessness of Luigi among all relatives. Some actually believed him and Luigi was cast as a villain and never invited for any social functions.

Anna's father survived another week. When Sonia told me this sad episode, she used the following words that do not translate very well in English,

"My wedding was more sorrowful than my father's funeral!"

Luigi and Sonia have a charming daughter, a fine combination of the good looks of both parents. Elio used to dislike her as a baby. The reason was that she took away the attention of his mother-in-law from his sons. He claimed that Anna's mother should only look after his sons. For a while he bothered Sonia and Luigi ruthlessly with phone calls and rude remarks when they met. On one occasion, Luigi would have punched Elio in face. Anna's mother intervened at that time but, for the two sisters, life had to take separate routes from that time onwards.

Sonia and Luigi left Rome in the end with their daughter, as soon as they found work near Turin. They had declared that they would not sit at the table with Elio or even be near him at any time. I have rarely seen them, as most of my visits were to Rome and Parma. I learnt it much later that Elio was one of the reasons for Anna and her brother Luca to leave Rome as well. The villain finally succeeded in getting everyone out of the way.

During the first few weeks, I had no idea about the darker side of Elio's character. I wondered, therefore, why everyone was shocked to see that I could put up with him. I did not obviously know enough about him at that time. I also did not wish to form a swift opinion about him and dismiss him altogether in our first few meetings. On the other hand, he offered to show me around and I found him not too disagreeable. I have heard some relatives express some sympathy for me. Some even put my behaviour down to the excessive peacefulness in my nature as an Indian!

During this trip, Anna suggested that we should visit her father's grave, which was some ten miles away from Rome. Elio offered to take us there, Anna, her brother Luca and me, on the anniversary of the death of Anna's father. The cemetery was a modern one and it had only a few separate plots for individual burials, presumably meant for very rich people. There were a number of shades with rows of concrete walls, 1.0 metre wide, 3.0 metres long and 4.0 metres tall. Each wall was divided into four compartments, some 800 mm square and 2.4 metres long, stacked vertically to form four individual graves, with a small projection in front to keep some flowers, candles, etc. It was very peaceful there and the place was kept clean and tidy.

My father-in-law was resting on the top floor of one such wall. Luca being the only son, stood in front of the grave and prayed and all of us knelt down behind him. Luca took a stick to dislodge the old flowers and replaced them with a new bunch and said that we should go back home. I felt that something was not right, as I mentally crossed the inter-religion divide. I decided that we had missed something in honouring the memories of my father-in-law. I asked Anna if we could get some step ladder. I am not sure if Elio heard what I said. He must have guessed from our expressions and the movement of hands I used as a sign for a step ladder. He patted me on my back and directed me away from Luca, who was quite bemused. I came to know later that he had to go to watch a football match! He murmured something that suggested insanity of his sister, who married such a slow-moving Indian!

We found an old man resting after his meal, who was presumably the "care-taker" of the establishment. It seemed to me as if he was not quite used to the company of the living! However, Elio convinced him that we needed a bucket of water, a brush, a drying cloth and a step ladder. He obliged and shook Elio's hand. I suspected that some Lira changed hands there!

I climbed the ladder and found the little balcony full of dirt and bird-droppings. I brushed it, cleaned it, rinsed it and wiped it until it showed the shine of the marble face. Elio left this to me since he had a bad back. By now, we had two other families watching us. The head-stone became so clean again that Anna could read the name standing on the floor, black letters on a shining white marble. It was then Anna's turn to outshine me. She dared to climb the unsteady ladder and arranged the flowers. The care-taker let us have some candles for a reasonable cost. The grave looked delightful!

When we finally finished, the spectators applauded and shook me by my hand and said something which was meant to express surprise and admiration. One of the older spectators thought that I was an Indian holy man! He said, like a true blue Italian, that it was the care-taker's job to keep the graves tidy and that everyone had gone corrupt and lazy, hence the state of the country, etc. Anna was watching with a hint of glistening in her eyes, that was enough for me as my reward.

The next step was our train journey in Italy. It is not an easy task for a stranger to plan a train journey in Italy. Elio knew how to find out about everything, filling the right forms, changes in time-table, supplements on various routes, etc. He used to travel a lot by train, to collect his favourite red wine, mushrooms, etc. from the countryside. Train travel was cheap in Italy and with his concessions as a government servant, Elio got the best out of it. He had some good experience in keeping things tidy and doing the work step-by-step, which came from his training at work. His handwriting was very good. If anyone in the family required any help with State-related matters, he would help right from filling in the necessary forms. With the complex and difficult government procedures in Italy, this was a very useful task he would do for others.

Elio was a very competent photographer. He used this skill to obtain a "Press" badge as a representative of a local news paper. This enabled him to attend many sports and competitions with a complimentary pass as a member of the Press. He took Carlo and me with him to see a few local games, which came as a welcome excuse for us to get out of the house, instead of participating (or pretending to do so) in endless conversations with the ladies!

Elio's company had some down-sides. He was an impatient driver and passing through red lights meant nothing more than a fine of some two thousand Lira. This was the case with many Italian drivers and driving in Rome seemed well above my capability.

Another aspect of Elio's character was his tendency to change abruptly from doing one thing and start something quite different. A chance to get close to a pretty young lady had the top priority in his actions. At an international table tennis tournament for juniors, I had spotted a good game involving Italian youngsters and sat down to watch it. Elio was supposed to take photos and do a report on this game for his local newspaper. Suddenly I realised that Elio had gone. I saw him in the balcony on the other side of the circular hall, chatting with the Russian ladies' team manager. He spent all afternoon taking photographs of her team. I never found out whether he really seduced women in this way or it was just playing about! Most of his in-laws believed that he did misbehave. For me, I did not think it was any of my business! On a few occasions, I felt sorry for him when he got a terse brush-off, although it did not seem to bother him at all.

I have met Elio during my various visits to Rome. In the early days, I was often amazed with his curiosity about matters that should not have concerned him. He had no regard for the rule about not asking a lady her age and a man his earnings. I benefited from the phrases my aunt Seeta often used. Answer to the query on salary was "enough to get by". Price of my house was "not too high". This was a version of the famous straight bat technique for defence employed by Geoffrey Boycott. I brought him down to his knees with such a classical defensive game. All he wanted to know was to place me according to my relative standing on his hierarchical ladder. Anna knew about his frustration from Carla and the sisters used to enjoy it very much.

Carla was prepared to be my disciple and receive training in dealing with Elio. She had to put up with a lot from him, his moaning about one thing or the other. One day, it was his back-trouble and, the other day, his Demo-Christian boss had made his life difficult because he was a socialist! I used to hear about the tantrums and many broken dishes in their household. This was understood to be a typical example of a loving relationship between Italian spouses.

Men would be thoroughly spoilt in their childhood by their mothers and grannies. A son could never do anything wrong in the eyes of an Italian mother. She would work hard at home and earn money to supplement the husband's salary, to dress her son properly and buy him all the toys he wanted. The shops took full advantage of this, as could be seen from the prices of children's clothes. I had a good experience of the affection bestowed by Indian mothers on their sons. But this would be nothing compared with the love and care of the Italian Mammas. Children could do what they liked in shops, on sea-shores and gardens. Nobody would dare to treat his little nephew or niece (as my uncle Hari did), or tap a boy on his head and call him by any names, in the presence of the child's mother in Italy. The offender would have his knuckles wrapped or his wrist slapped by the lady-protector of the child, if not some other part of his anatomy!

Elio had come out of the comfort of his mamma and entered the shadow of his wife, where he wished to remain protected and looked after all the time. They would of course have arguments but only to enhance the bond. This is believed to be the case generally about many Italian couples. Their love was not reduced by their occasional fling and extra-marital affairs, as I had seen with Angela earlier. Marcello Mastroianni, the famous film star, had a child by Genevieve Bujold and Signora Mastroianni did not think it was serious enough to go for a divorce! This might seem to be the extreme, but I believe that Italian women know their men thoroughly. They have measured them up to the last millimetre and they know their inability to look after themselves, their fallibility and their vulnerable character. This makes the ladies confident about their men coming back to the fold and home comforts, sooner rather than later, after any temporary aberration of the romantic kind..

I have had unusually good fortune in being in the good books with ladies from my Italian family connection. Perhaps they found me more mature than the likes of Elio, or harmless as he often hinted in his childish way. Some ladies seemed to like me for my dark complexion. One spinster even said openly that she would have got married if she were to meet someone with complexion as dark as mine. I felt flattered and so did Anna! I wondered why people in some countries made such a fuss and discriminated against all non-white people! Anna's brother was quite content that his sister should marry an Indian Hindu but his generosity did not extend far enough to condone the attention I received from so many Italian females. He developed a different theory based on what he had read in a little book about India. I heard him say that the Indians worship cows and, therefore, the women with brains like cows must like Indian men! This was an unkind remark on intelligence of Italian women, which did not help his standing among the female folk.

Elio's moral values did not seem to conflict with his religious believes. He was not a religious person, any way. He was a socialist, an opponent of the allegedly corrupt Demo-Christians and their Mafia connection. He once asked me if I was a Catholic. When I said I was not, he assumed that I must be a Protestant. When he knew that I was a Hindu, he seemed to have warmed up a little more towards me, like many other relatives. They wanted to know about my religion and I obliged them as well as my limited Italian would permit. On one of my later visits, I took some photographs of older women, Vahini, Dadaji's wife, and my aunt Seeta, dressed up in all their glory, gold necklaces and rich coloured saris with borders woven with threads of gold. They were fascinated with the ornaments and saris. Next time, I took some silk scarves and necklaces with black beads woven in gold thread, a typical ornament for a married woman. My popularity index must have jumped a few points!

In my opinion, the line dividing good and bad moral standards shifts up or down in different countries. In Mumbai, not all men were like saints. For example, Nanaji and Doctor were strictly religious but they had sought extra-marital adventures of one sort or the other. I would find it hard to condemn Elio for his shortfalls of any kind. He really believed that he should go and get what he could, without worrying about anyone's opinion. He was often critical of the Catholic religion, not for its principles written in the Bible but for what people, politicians and priests did in the name of religion. I would have found it hypocritical to tell him about the superiority of Indian moral standards, based on stories from Ramayana and Mahabharata. We held the same opinion that the behaviour of followers of the religion should be considered as a measure of the effectiveness of what their religion might have preached.

I consider it my good fortune to have met different people from parts of the world other than the country of my origin. It has enabled me to re-examine my own values against those of others, accounting for the different background and evolution of various practices. It must be futile to judge other people unfairly and on the basis of one's own surroundings, which may well have been the starting points of conflicts in many parts of the world.

13
Macalister

I knew John Macalister for the first time in 1979, during my short stay at Portsmouth as a resident engineer on one of the Naval base projects. He was appointed by the Government Department to oversee the project work. He might have been some fifty years of age at that time. He was born and brought up in Glasgow, where he had worked in the construction business most of his life. He was a typically resilient Scotsman, who would try his hand at anything instead of remaining without work. However, even he had to give up trying to make a living in Glasgow, when the building industry had very bad time in that part of the UK. To escape from such cold winds blowing in the private sector, he decided to take shelter in the Government service. He eventually came to Portsmouth on transfer.

John Macalister

John Macalister's father was a civil servant. He had got married rather late to a girl much younger than him. John was born when his father was some forty-five years of age. Unfortunately, John's mother had a brief illness and died when John was eight years old. John's father loved his wife and John so much that he did not marry again. His unmarried elder sister stayed with him and looked after John. By the time John was sixteen, his aunt was taken ill. She had to be taken to hospital where she died after some six months. John's father wanted him to study and qualify as a professional. John could not bear the thought of leaving his father on his own at that stage. He decided that they had to be a proper family soon. His solution was to get married as soon as possible. He had a childhood sweetheart, Betty, who lived in the same neighbourhood and the two families knew each other very well. At the age of nineteen, soon after he finished his secondary school studies, John got a job as an apprentice with a local building firm. The next thing he did was to get married.

There was every indication that the Macalisters would have lived happily for a long time. Within a year or so, John's father was looking forward to becoming a grandfather. They were reasonably well off and plans were made to buy a bigger house and so on. But this was not to be and the real script turned out to be quite different. John's father developed heart trouble and died after a brief illness. Betty was having a difficult pregnancy. As the young couple were recovering from the shock of the death of John's father, Betty gave birth to a boy prematurely. The boy was born with heart problems and lived only for six months. It was too much for the young mother to bear. She became ill and developed asthma. After some hospital treatment, she was destined to have medication for the rest of her life. Doctors also told her that she could not have children any more. Life could not have been more unfair for John and Betty. I often wondered why god-fearing and decent men like John should suffer this way, just like some similar situations I had known about in India earlier.

Like many men of courage, John had picked himself up and adopted his niece, Jane, and brought her up as if she was his own daughter. Jane's father had left John's sister for a younger woman. Jane's mother could not bear with the misfortune and died when Jane was only eight years of age. Since that time, Betty looked after her. Jane was a clever girl. She got her degree and qualified as a teacher. Later on, she got a job in a school in Portsmouth, married a young man working in the Navy and settled in the same town.

Transfer to Portsmouth was quite suitable for John since Jane lived there. She had a spare granny suite in her house where Betty and John could live quite comfortably. We lived on the same estate in a rented flat, which was adequate for the three of us, my wife Anna, our daughter Asha and me. Betty would be more comfortable in Portsmouth, the climate being warmer and drier than that in Glasgow. Jane's husband worked as a chef in the Navy, away from the Naval base for most of the year. Jane worked part-time in the local school. Betty was well enough to look after Julie and Lisa, Jane's daughters, some seven and thirteen years of age respectively. During the daytime, it would help Jane to have someone like Betty at home, to look after the girls after school until she came back from work.

Macalister had come to our office on the first day of my starting work. We introduced ourselves and he said to me in his Scottish accent,

"Welcome to Portsmouth, Laddie!"

There was a ripple of laughter, coming from the direction of the typing pool. This was on account of Macalister's version of the name "Portsmouth". Instead of pronouncing the ending after "Ports" as "muth", as preferred by the locals, the Scots tend to give it the full treatment and say "mouth"! In the first meeting, he told me to call him Macalister, mainly because there were so many by the name "John". He disliked being called "Jack" or "Jock" and even claimed to be proud of his surname, which was typical of those from the Clan he belonged. Some people called him Mac but he persuaded me to address him by the full name, as he thought I pronounced it in the most proper manner, far better than the locals or cockneys did. For him, everyone south of York was a cockney. He was proud of his family tradition and bravery of his ancestors who had fought in the first world-war. His accents fascinated me and I understood him quite clearly, as opposed to the problems I had with other Glaswegians, Billy Connolly for example. I tried to copy the way he rolled the sound of the letter "R" and pronounced the words with longer vowels, like "two" and "doomed", reminiscent of the "Dad's Army" actor John Laurie.

Macalister soon came to know that I lived in the same neighbourhood as he did. He also knew that I had a girl of seven years of age, almost as old as his granddaughter Julie, whom he loved most dearly. He told me that Jane could help us if we needed anything and promised to bring Julie to our flat during the next weekend. I found this quite contrary to our neighbours in London. They had been somewhat cold towards us and mixed with us when it suited them, in a limited sense. We did find playmates for Asha eventually but I was a little worried for Asha in Portsmouth. Her first few days at the school were a little difficult. Asha's school had children from Naval officers' families. Most of them seemed somewhat unruly to me. This might have been the result of their fathers being away on Naval duties and this could have adversely affected the home discipline. It also seemed that the children believed that their fathers were involved in the defence of the country and that this gave them a special status. They had probably seen films where the male soldiers behaved in a macho manner and the women with more freedom than their civilian counterparts. The youngsters seemed to believe that it was their entitlement to behave similarly, keeping with the family tradition. I got the impression that the teachers condoned the behaviour of such children.

Macalister came with Julie to our home as agreed. Julie was very pretty indeed and I could see why Macalister was so very fond of her. I could not take my eyes off her myself. She had dark blue eyes and golden hair. She must be blessed by the Gods with a smile that was simply unique. When she smiled, which she did quite often, the smile showed for a split-second in her eyes and on her lips. Her eyes lit up and her lips parted just enough to show the pearl-like teeth, as if they were set so regularly by a gifted goldsmith. Her smile could inspire a poet sitting by a lakeside, to compare it with a quick flash of lightning in the blue sky and its reflection in the clear lake in front! Julie used to visit us regularly after school every afternoon. The highlight of my weekend was to open the door for her on Saturday mornings. It started my day beautifully, when she came and stood at the threshold an asked me if Asha would come out to play with her, with that exclusive and angelic smile of hers.

My employers were soon tasked with examination of old buildings in the dockyard. The intention was to decide whether to demolish them or repair them for some alternative use. This was required by the Government policy to reduce the Naval base activities and rationalise the use of real estate in the dockyard. Portsmouth as a town seemed to be steeped with tradition to me. The old ships, the brave admirals and the sea-faring reminded me of my ancestors in Mumbai. If a stranger were to meet any elderly people in the city, they would often give an account of some anecdotes revealing details of the unique and rich historical past. It seemed wrong that the place should risk losing its glory and character, because of the decline of the dockyard, its main source of employment and generating associated business.

The city of Portsmouth was known for people skilled in building ships and specialist work like welding copper pipes that had to be fitted in the limited space inside a submarine. This was a very complex three-dimensional task. These skills had been passed on from generation to generation. Besides, young welders had their training in the pipe-shop, which was perhaps unique to Portsmouth. This building was one of those buildings under examination. I had prepared a proposal to have the building strengthened, with the addition of bracings to the structure. This would enable partitioning of the building and using a part of it for other functions transferred from elsewhere, while keeping half of it to continue the training of pipe-welders and electricians. One day, I spent quite some time explaining merits of my case to the authorities. At the end of the day, I was so tired that I stopped at a pub for a beer on my way back home.

I was just about to sit down with my glass before I felt a heavy hand on my back. Macalister was behind me with another man.

"Well done, Laddie!"

Macalister said with his booming voice.

"Meet Ron Grant, the shop-steward of the Electricians' Union and an electric engineer. He was telling me all about your good work, helping to save the pipe-shop."

It was to remain a mystery for me and I never found out how Ron came to know about my pipe-shop report. He shook my hand and laughed like Danny Kaye in the film Merry Andrews. He resembled Danny Kaye a little, with his sharp nose, his immaculate dress and his manner of speaking. He spoke in an excited manner about how my report may keep the pipe-shop going and with it, the training of young welders. For Ron, who had started his life as a trainee electrician and technician in the dockyard, demolition of the pipe-shop would have been most unwelcome. He was nearing retirement and it would please him very much that some training could be kept up in the dockyard.

I tried to tell him that my report was based on engineering judgement and cost-effectiveness in planning the future functions of the dockyard. He exclaimed,

"Ha, ha ha! An honest Indian, Eh! Have a glass of port on me; that will freshen you up!"

I suddenly remembered a very skilled draftsman from Mumbai, Kadrekar by name. I was working by his side during my training days. He was a small man but as sharp-featured as Ron and well dressed albeit in Indian clothes. His personality matched his work, neat and perfect. His engineering drawings looked so artistic that they could be framed as paintings. He taught me some skills in planning a drawing on a 800 x 1200 mm size paper. He used to say,

"Desai, all parts of the drawing should be in harmony with each other and made to look like a composition. Work should be in perfect plumb! No helter-skelter business, understand?"

When he thought my drawing was all right, he used to suggest a few minor adjustments. Finally, he used to pat me on my back and say,

"Not bad, not bad at all! Have a sniff of my snuff, it is good for refreshing your brain!"

People like me, who leave their countries and move elsewhere, would often look for some resemblance of things of the past with those in their new surroundings. Some parallels with the old places and people seem to provide a relief and reduce the strangeness of the new place. Kadrekar's snuff seemed to have reappeared in the form of Ron's glass of port for me. It did relieve my strain of the day and I went home a happy man.

Ron and Macalister had known each other for many years. Macalister often said that Ron was among the few Englishmen who were good company at the bar. Ron was a widower and he had no children of his own. He had adopted two orphan girls who were now married and they were as dear to Ron as his own children might have been. Ron's daughters knew Jane very well. This little group of ladies provided Anna with the sort of company women need in a strange town. I used to go to work, where I had enough worries and people around me. For Anna to be on her own would have been hard without these ladies.

Ron, Macalister and I became good friends. They helped me a lot with my work as well. I was neither a Union man nor did I have any interest in politics. I have always been a conservative with small "c" but Ron thought that I belonged to the right. On the other hand, Macalister knew about my background. Just like me, he had always earned his living and supported his family with hard work. All the same, Ron and Macalister often did me a big favour by lobbying successfully with the dockyard staff and avoiding any strong reactions to some of the construction proposals. They believed in me and I always gave them my honest professional opinion on matters of non-confidential nature.

We often joked about the British Empire, Ron claiming that people like my forefathers must have kept it going as long as it did. He had heard from me about Nanaji and Mr Bailey. I used to say that the British people like him and Macalister were responsible for the longevity of the Empire. They created trust in the fairness of the system among Indians, which made a lasting impression on the common people, in spite of the cruelty of those like General Dyer. Nevertheless, the conversation never got really serious, as Ron invariably gave his Danny Kaye laughter and offered me a glass of port!

All three of us had one thing in common, which was our faith in God. We believed in our individual ways of worship although not dismissing others as irrelevant. Both Ron and Macalister loved Christian religion. Macalister often claimed that his faith was the only thing that kept him going. I found him very positive in his religious beliefs and very open-minded about other religions. He knew that there were other well-developed ways of worshipping the God and never derided rituals other than those in the Christian Church. He believed that there was only one God but He was available to all creatures. He used to make fun of some old writings in the scriptures and wondered if they could be modernised. His favourite one was the commandment,

"Thou shalt not covet thy neighbour's ass".

He would rather reword it to replace the word "ass" by an "E-type Jaguar", his favourite model of a car.

Macalister tried to teach me Contract Bridge and succeeded up to a point. We played as a family on a few occasions, with Betty and Anna as our partners. However, Betty and Anna would rather talk and not play with full concentration. Once there was a serious incident. Betty had the King of Hearts but she did not play it when I tried a finesse, playing the Queen from Anna's dummy hand. Macalister was furious but controlled himself. Betty had just forgotten the basic rules, while eating her yoghurt and talking to Anna! That was the end of our family sessions of Contract Bridge.

Macalister believed that Contract Bridge was a perfect model for real life. You are dealt with some cards and you must make the best out of them. You have a partner and the two of you have to develop the perfect understanding. Conducting the game is a very skilled and responsible job, playing the cards as a partner of the team that has the successful bid. You must take risks and take chances with a fall-back position to avoid total disaster. Some cards are such that, when making a no-trump bid, you have to discard your higher cards, and even aces, in some suits, to unblock a winning suit. I had the experience of this in real life, when it was most desirable to discard some things that appeared valuable but they were blocking the path towards achieving the final result.

Macalister and Betty had discarded many of their own activities and fully involved themselves in looking after Julie and Lisa. They reminded me of Anna's uncle Gino and aunt Nella. Lisa was a girl who wanted to grow quickly. She was fourteen but looked nearly seventeen. She was very good-looking but she was too keen to beautify herself with make-up and dresses. Eyes turned when she walked her dog every morning and evening. She knew she was attractive and walked in a manner that was meant to attract attention. I do not believe people when they say that all girls are innocent creatures. I have seen some girls in Asha's school group together and treat girls outside their group in a way as cruelly as the beasts in the jungle. Lisa was no angel with Julie and often treated her like a little slave. Julie, on the other hand, adored her big sister. In this context, one instance has remained deep in my memory.

One morning on a Saturday, I came home with Asha at about 11.00 am after a morning session of table-tennis practice games. I saw Julie sitting all by herself on the steps of her home. I asked her what the matter was. I thought that she was waiting for Asha to come back and play with her. I asked her to come with us. She raised her sad blue eyes, curled her lips and said,

"No thank you, uncle! I would rather stay here. My mummy has gone out with Granny Betty and Grandpa John. Lisa is playing cards with her friends. I wanted to join them but they let me play for only ten minutes. Lisa said that I couldn't play well enough and asked me to go out. It is a good game and I would like to learn. Perhaps they will call me back if one of the girls wants to go out. What if Lisa calls me and I am not here?"

Tears came to my eyes! I remembered Sulu all of a sudden and my own childhood days. I would not want to experience that again!

I did not adore Julie just because of her good looks. She had a voice like that produced by gently plucking the strings of a Sitar. She had what they call a "presence", whereby everything would look brighter when she was around and the atmosphere was charmed when she said something. She was so delicate that she could have perched on rose petals and decorated the flower. She was different to the other children in the neighbourhood with their fathers working for the Navy. These boys and girls were spoilt and quite rough as I have described earlier. Julie was influenced by Macalister and Betty, who were ideal grandparents. Jane was loving but she believed equally in discipline. Her father's absence from home was more than compensated by the rest of the family. Julie trusted me as Macalister's friend, with a sweet mixture of respect and affection.

Julie and Asha got on very well together. Taking the girls to school and school activities would be done in turns by both families. Both mothers used to treat them well, let them visit and play with each other as often as possible and arrange functions like birthdays together. Betty was a great granny figure, despite her ill health. Macalister used to enjoy all this to the full! The only time the situation changed was when Jane's husband, Alexander or Sandy, came home on shore leave. During this time, Asha and Julie's other friends would not visit her home. One day, Asha happened to touch one of his Navy shields. Although there was no damage, Sandy said something unpleasant. From that time, we decided that Asha should not visit Julie when Sandy was around.

Macalister had developed a strict routine during the time Sandy was at home. He would stay with Betty in their room most of the time after work. On Sundays, he would go to the church and, thereafter, he mostly went to Ron's house, with Jane and the girls. I was surprised with this to start with, knowing the importance of the Sunday lunch for British families. It took me some time to figure it out on my own, as I could not ask Jane or Macalister about such sensitive family matter.

There was no question of my conversation with Sandy. He would exchange greetings like "Good Morning" without raising his head and seeing me eye to eye. He was a peculiar character in appearance. His hair must have been blond when he was younger. With age, however, it was getting very thin on the top. He used to hide his bald patch by turning his side hair up and perhaps sticking everything in place with some hair-cream. He walked with smaller steps than normal men would do. I noticed the number of rings he wore on his fingers and all this did not seem quite normal to me. I could not stand him really and any conversation seemed rather impossible for me. Macalister used to change his voice when Sandy was mentioned in any of his conversation between Ron and myself. It was clear that he wished to avoid any immodest remark.

One Sunday afternoon, I heard some loud conversation among men and laughter when I was passing Sandy's home with Anna. I said to her that he must be a lucky man. His wife had cooked the roast dinner, taken the girls somewhere else and he was enjoying the Sunday afternoon with his mates. It suddenly occurred to me that it was fair enough that the host should have cleared the coast and sent the girls away. But what about the guests? My idea of a party was based on our days at the Linguist Club and Manfred's organisation of right mixture of young men and women. The common convention was to have one invitation for two guests, for him and for her.

Anna raised her eyebrows, just as she did when she had to display her superiority. She spoke to me in a low voice, in a manner meant to make me feel uneasy about having asked a silly question,

"You won't understand these things! This is a party for special type of Navy people, for men only."

I was not convinced. I asked Macalister at a suitable time what was the matter with Sandy. He touched the left side of his nose with the index finger of his left hand. He said that Sandy had lost interest in women and mixed parties! I felt as if someone had switched on a hundred watt bulb in my brain and I was seeing what I would abhor. I was stunned with the thought that a man with such beautiful family should opt for such life-style.

I felt like an old Indian and wondered why Jane might have married this reprobate of a man called Sandy. She was educated, beautiful and from a good family. Sandy looked quite a mismatch for her. Perhaps the God may not be too keen to have perfectly matching pairs, any way. What would happen if the nasty men were all married to nasty women? It would not be much good if weak men also had wives of weak character. I have heard a philosopher friend of mine say that without Xantipee as his wife, Socrates would not have become one of the greatest philosophers!

Perhaps a girl like Jane, living on her own in Portsmouth far away from her home in Glasgow and the Macalisters, might have acted in a way that seemed appropriate to her at that time. Betty had brought up Jane to bear no grudge against her own father who had deserted her mother and her. Jane might have considered herself fortunate to have people like the Macalisters to look after her during her childhood. Psychologically, she could even have thought of repaying their debt through her own action. This might have meant helping some vulnerable young man and making his life worthwhile with the strength she had acquired by coping with her own adversities. Sandy might well have had the guile to draw out the mother in her and he might have won her sympathy with some sad stories. Moreover, even an ass would look like a pedigree race-horse in the smart Naval uniform. I should not be less than generous to Sandy but I could see why Jane may have undertaken to complete her mission, even after she might have known more about her husband within a few months of marriage.

In 1983, Ron took early retirement went to Australia to stay with his nephew. Both Macalister and I were really sorry. However, it was soon time for me to leave Portsmouth as well. In spite of everybody's efforts, some buildings in the dockyard were demolished. The pipe-shop survived, but only just! It was an amazing turn of the wheel of fortune that the Falkland conflict arose at that time. The Argentinean dictator Gualtieri helped to achieve in 1982 what the Unions could not achieve during the earlier years. The authorities stopped staff cuts and restored some activities in the dockyard. People like Macalister were striving to prepare warships with the help of workers who had received retrenchment notices. One could feel the patriotism of the workers and I had the first hand experience of the greatness of Great Britain!

Soon after I left Portsmouth, I heard that Macalister had got angina. I met him again at Portsmouth after about one year. Sandy had left his job in the Navy and become a prison officer. Macalister must have found it difficult to carry on with him around all the time. Lisa had gone away to college in Nottingham. Julie had grown up enough to look after herself after school. Macalister felt that Betty was no longer needed and that her health had improved sufficiently for them to move back to Glasgow. He made up his mind to take early retirement, packed up and went back to Glasgow.

Next time I met Macalister was after some eight years and in Glasgow. My next job involved some travelling and, particularly in the North and in Scotland. I wrote a letter to Macalister at his Glasgow address to say that I planned to visit a place called Beith on a certain day. He wrote back and we arranged to meet. He looked rather old for his age and I knew the reason why. Betty had passed away. I felt sorry for him when he told me that he no longer had any reason for remaining fit and well. My reminiscing the old times cheered him up a little. Lisa had got married and she lived in Birmingham. Julie was growing prettier day by day and she had done very well at the GCSE examination. Perhaps she would go to Cambridge. Macalister was very fond of her, much more than me, of course. All had turned out well for Jane's family.

I came home and told Anna about my meeting with Macalister. Asha was listening. She asked about Julie, her childhood friend. Asha had also grown into a fine young lady. I treated her like a friend, as the Indian rule went. Children after Sixteen years of age must be treated as equals! My good friend asked me an awkward question.

"Babbo, tell me the truth. You didn't love Julie more than you loved me when we were in Portsmouth. Yes?"

I felt a chill and perspiration in the small of my back. But I quickly recovered and said quite convincingly,

"Of course not, dear! She was nice but she was just a neighbour. You have been and will always be our treasure!"

14.
Summing up

*I*n the foregoing chapters , I have described some major events and given pen-pictures of the main characters whom I met from time to time. These events and people had significant influence on me, both during the time I spent in Mumbai and during the first few years of my life in the UK. I would like to mention some other events and encounters that could help me to sum up the process of my transition from a resident of Mumbai into a citizen of the UK.

I believe that an urge to communicate properly in any language has been among the important parts of my character. In this respect, my mother-tongue, Marathi, comes first, followed by English and then Indian languages. I really believe that one must not look down upon one's mother-tongue. Those who do so are likely to be disadvantaged when they try to learn other languages. It might seem ironic that I do not speak Marathi or Hindi on a regular basis but the standard of my Marathi and Hindi could be higher than many Indians living in the UK. I owe this to Dadaji's influence and memories of Mirzasaab. I love to speak Marathi and do so whenever I can, with people that are willing and able to speak in Marathi. I remember a colleague with Marathi surname, who worked with me during my early days in the UK. I greeted him in Marathi but he did not exchange my greetings. I did not think much about it but he insisted on telling me that he stopped speaking Marathi as soon as he stepped out of his home. I heard him speak a little Marathi later on with another person, which was appalling. The sentences started with badly pronounced Marathi words and ended similarly, with the gaps filled in English! One day, after we got to know each other a little better, he probably wanted to make up with me. He said that he had a son, eight years of age, and he had started teaching him some Marathi. I was not in a generous mood and I told him that, for the sake of his beloved son, he should stop doing so. When he insisted and asked me why, I told him with a straight face that he spoke Marathi so badly that it would be a disservice to my mother-tongue. It would also ruin his son's chances of learning Marathi well in the future, having made such a bad start. He never spoke to me again.

I have often regretted that my children are not able to speak Marathi. It is my fault that I could never teach anyone. All the same, I was hoping that they would use their mother-tongue, Italian, when speaking with their mother. They have studied Italian up to GCSE level but they would speak only in English at home. I checked with others, including those with German or Spanish as their first language, whether they had any different experience. It seems that all children like to speak only in English, once they start attending schools. Later on, I realised that this was generally true with children belonging to all ethnic minority families, with mixed marriages or otherwise, Indians or other Asians or even Europeans. I know that there are some Urdu, Tamil and Chinese week-end schools dedicated to promoting these languages among school children. But this will only postpone the assimilation of future generations in the English-speaking mass and not prevent it for ever.

Irrespective of the fact that they may dispense with the use of Indian languages, second and future generation people of Indian origin are likely to be brought up with good discipline. At present, they have a reputation as keen students. This is shown by the percentage of university students of Indian origin, which is about twenty-five percent, while there are only some five percent people of Indian descent in the UK. If they are able to believe that they have good opportunities to achieve their full potential, they could become a valuable asset to the future of this country.

Just as the youngsters wish to be identified with their peers at school, the adults also should make a deliberate effort to be in harmony with the indigenous population. This may be more easy to say than to put in practice. It is true that all indigenous people may not be interested in reaching out to an Indian-looking person. In many cases, the first encounter could make an Indian person feel unwanted and dread another similar experience. In my opinion, one ought to forget the first hurdles of this nature and, if possible, try to keep an open mind. I have always believed that there should be a will to achieve what one believes to be desirable, not just for one's own sake but for the future.

On balance, the process of learning my steps in the western world was not so painful. I have had more direct contact with the western way of life than some UK Indians of my age, who have chosen to live in a circle of Indian friends and relatives only. This was my choice, which might not have been much better or far worse than the one made by other people of Indian origin. I am also content to have maintained a certain standard of the Marathi and Hindi languages, although I could not pass on these languages to the next generation.

Just as most religions start off on the right track and deviate in the future under the influence of political and economical forces, human behaviour can change and relationships can undergo similar stages. One starts off well with the initial enthusiasm but to sustain the same momentum and direction is difficult, unless one has very strong base and deep roots. In my case, my relationship with Elio could not be maintained. We did not quarrel but I decided to steer clear of any controversy. I had noticed his tendency to line up people in hierarchical order. Gradually with time, I came to know about his unkindness to Anna in the past, when he tried to take over the household after my father-in-law died. He started pestering my mother-in law and tried to force her to decide that Anna should not continue her study and she must go to work. Anna was good at French and very keen on English. She wanted to become a bilingual secretary and enrol for an entry examination. However, Elio's sister had failed this examination twice and he could not bear the thought of Anna passing it! He also had a plan whereby Anna should remain unmarried, support her mother and ensure that his sons would be well looked after for a long time. He made Anna's life so difficult that her widowed mother could not do much about it. She must have been torn between her love for Carla and her sons on one side and her duty towards Anna on the other. In the end Anna decided to go to London, to pursue the study of English language and seek a career later in Rome. Her mother could do no more than give her money and her blessings.

Elio became more and more anxious about my progress in my career and his initial curiosity was replaced by mild jealousy. I came to know some Professors at the University of Rome, who were like Gods to him, and he could not bear the thought that I could be on equal terms with them. As his sons grew older, he started concerning himself about my daughter's progress. Since Anna was Carla's inferior, Anna's children should not surpass Carla's children! It was a warped logic and I became disgusted with it. In the end, he moved away from Rome and I did not hear from him again. Anna has kept in touch with her sister and the boys, which is good enough for me. The reader will understand the reason for my using past tense about him in my narrative. In my way of dealing with relatives, there is no room for a quarrel and remaining aloof is as far as I would go with any of my relatives.

I truly regret my loss of warm relationship with Anna's Mamma. She came to our home to stay for a long time when Asha was a baby. She was

My mother-in-law with Asha

supposed to come to help during Anna's pregnancy but Asha was born two weeks early. However, whenever she was with us, she would want me to ensure that Anna got enough rest and that I took care of both, Anna and Asha. Perhaps she must have thought too highly of my abilities! I did not mind being told this way but the problem came when Asha was four years of age. She started having an influence on her, which made me uncomfortable. I began to suspect that Asha would grow up a mentally weak child with all that pampering. While it might have been all right in Italy, it could not be so in the UK, with the competitive world that we have. With Asha's mixed parentage, she would have added problems and she needed to be strong-minded to face them. Furthermore, she started expressing some anti-English opinions. I was conscious of the fact that whatever we had in London, it was our world and we had to make our life within our environment.

Another strand in my Italian connection concerned Anna's brother, Luca. He got a job and moved to Asti, probably to escape from Elio's influence. At Asti, he met a very pretty and clever girl, called Luisa. Her mother, Oliva, was a formidable lady with a very strong character. She was methodical, strict and very set in her ways. She had a difficult life after her husband's death. Luisa and her brother were looked after single-handedly by Oliva. Luisa's brother was an adventurous young man, a motor-cycle enthusiast. He used to take part in speed-riding competitions. Unfortunately, he was seriously injured at one such event and died at a very young age. Oliva must have taken this blow very badly, but she managed to bear it with courage. In the end, Luisa did very well at studies, graduated and got a good job. She was another of the young ladies, who must take on the mission of improving a young man's lot! Luisa helped Luca to complete his studies, before they got married. Rumour has it that Oliva was also a great influence in bringing Luca in line. I remember Luca and Luisa as a good couple, blessed with the sound support of Oliva. Very soon, Oliva was a proud Nonna of little twin girls. Anna's mother was over the moon too and used to sing Luisa's praise, her beauty, intelligence, etc. However, the two mothers were totally different in character. Anna's mother had other grandchildren from her daughters while Oliva had only one daughter, two granddaughters and their home as her own home. Oliva had her rules for bringing up the little girls, which were closer to mine than those of Anna's mother. Anna's mother must have said something and Oliva could not put up with it. Like a lioness defending her lair, she told Luca to choose between her and his mother. That was that and the twin girls were shadowed by only one grandmother thereafter, Oliva. Anna was furious and told me about this, giving me an impression that Oliva behaved like an insensitive monster. It was natural for her to react that way but I made the mistake of taking Oliva's side, which I thought was defensible. Because of my tactlessness and Anna's decision to report it to her mother, my standing with Anna's mother became very low. She never came again on long visits to London, believing that I wished to keep my children out of her influence.

Apart from the lot of young persons of Indian origin, I have had some concern about some older people. In India, an old man or a woman would be treated as an asset. My mother's mother, Nani, and my aunt, Seeta, were invaluable to their families. My grandfather, Nanaji, and Dadaji were respected by the younger people generally and revered by their families. Their advice was always gratefully received. In short, they were never a burden for anybody. I despair of the condition of some elderly Indians here, whom I have seen as rather desolate and lonely. They go and play cards in some clubs and have a group of their own and spend time somewhat in a sorry state, as if waiting for God.

Baby-sitting was never a problem in Mumbai. My brothers, our sister and I were often looked after by elderly relatives and neighbours when we were young. In London, when Asha was about one year old, we went to see a baby-sitter's place and found it utterly depressing. Children were made to sit on chairs or lie on the floor, with a very unfriendly lady nearby, watching television. We heard stories about nappies not changed and an unruly child being kept tied up, etc. I knew an Egyptian family who gave us another address, where their little boy attended. When Anna and I went there, by coincidence, the boy was led away by an uncouth man and he addressed his ward as "little wog". The other kids laughed. That was decision time for us. What will my mother think of such child-minders? Anna's mother, who was like a goddess of love, will never forgive us if her granddaughter were to be left in such hands. I put my hand on Anna's back and led her away, pushing Asha's pram as quickly as possible. I promised her that, even if we had to starve, our children will never be with such strangers. She had the grace to take the only choice available to us and agreed to stay at home, even if it meant sacrificing her own career.

Anna had two more daughters, Lina in 1974 and Seema in 1980. Lina was born with a mental handicap. She has been a slow learner and with very limited academic abilities. The first year was a difficult one. People told us all sorts of horror stories about life with children like Lina. But we got over the difficult times, mostly because of Anna's strength of mind. Lina has progressed well in most cases other than academic study. Her health is good and she loves music and sports. There could not be many youngsters as passionate about the programme "Star-Trek" as Lina. She knows most of them almost by heart! I remember most dearly her playing five-a-side football match for mentally handicapped children at Wembley stadium. She scored a goal, tackled a boy one and a half times her size and was booked by the referee. I have a video to prove it and I often boast that a member of my family has played at Wembley! At least she has helped me to remain down to earth and, perhaps, kept us united as a family. I remember her keeping me company during the time I was doing part-time study for my doctorate and when I worked on my thesis at home. She used to sit next to me and help me with the printing the draft. She would remind me of the screen break I had to take and even make me a cup of tea. She would say something quite different and silly, which distracted me and kept me going. I wonder what I would have done without her!

Lina, Seema and Satish

Seema means "horizon" or limit in Marathi. She came a little late in our lives and her birth restored Anna's confidence, which was shaken a little when Lina was born. While she represents a full stop as far of the size of our family is concerned, she has been brilliant and, so far, she has surpassed everything achieved by anyone in our family. By God's grace, I hope that there is more to come in the future. The joy of having her and seeing her grow up with her sisters has been limitless.

I made my journey from East to West, not without difficulties and with some help from a few good people as I have described, in the UK and in Italy. It all seems worthwhile so far and all the past hurts and difficulties could be forgiven and forgotten. My adopted country did continue to reward me further. I was awarded a doctorate for my research at the age of fifty-six. In February 1998, I was invited to the Buckingham Palace to receive my OBE from Her Majesty the Queen, which I shall cherish all my life. For me personally, these events represent the most important stage of the joyful second part of my life, which started in 1968!

I am sure that there is more to come my way, as I intend to carry on with my journey for some time!

Satish and Anna

15
Epilogue

*F*rom the narration of events and sketches of characters I have presented so far, the reader may have had a fair idea about the key people I have met. However, my experience concerns the time I spent some thirty years ago in a small part of the world and it may not be relevant to the issues of the modern world. My stories are limited to some unique circumstances. I could not make any generalised observation based on them, since it would be as unreliable as a graph plotted by extrapolating some modest data. Some pointers provided by my narratives could nevertheless assist me in looking at issues that are relevant to the present world and the future generations of people, especially those with background similar to my own.

My first difficulties at school started with the limitation on human knowledge. I was concerned that we could not find out anything definite about the beginning of the world or even about conception of life. There are some theories about this now, but not much has been found that can be accepted as the whole truth.

As a student, I never believed the stories about the role of a stork in arrival of a baby. I did not believe that the position of planets or constellations at the time of birth could influence human life. My uncle Hari would have disagreed, but the birth of a child could not possibly bring bad luck or cause illness to any other member of the family. One of my relatives had a girl with a deformed leg. Her mother-in-law believed that conception on a no-moon day could affect the formation of a baby! We thought that this was rather an unkind thing to say and it could not have any scientific basis. I believed that the birth of a child should result from union of a couple, symbolising their love and willingness to have a baby.

I was reasonably sure about the conception of animal life. However, this is no longer the case today! The present arguments start at the embryonic stage. Conception of human life can happen outside the mother's body and embryos can be "frozen" successfully. Human organs and even the heart, a symbol of love, can be produced in a laboratory! We have not found out, however, whether such a baby would have any deficiency rooted in the depth of its inner being, while its external body may look like other human babies. This is the part of knowledge outside the human reach, as I had come to understand in my childhood days.

We talk about the blood-cells, DNA and genes, but we don't know all the constituents of the body and soul combination. Personally, I was unpleasantly surprised to hear about "Dolly", the Edinburgh ewe produced by cloning. I would be worried whether the meat of such sheep would contain some ingredients that may be unnatural and undesirable for human consumption. The news about her producing a lamb was even more alarming. I had hoped that, like mules, the clones would not reproduce. The creation of Dolly should have remained as a one-off experiment, so that the lambs would continue to be produced from normal sheep. Any future development of cloning technique to produce human beings really worries me.

Another aspect of child-birth could be the state of the mother's mind during pregnancy. If a baby is not wanted by the mother, should a mother have an abortion? In my narration about Nanaji's times, I have mentioned the plight of an unfortunate unmarried mother. This lady gave her baby away at the holy place in India. Would such babies have any poisonous influence on their mind, resulting from their mothers' agonies during their pregnant days? Would it remain dormant and reappear in future generations? If this is true, there may be a problem hidden in the form of succeeding generations of non-white Americans, born as a result of rapes on black slave girls committed by their white masters.

From the very early days in the life of a child, it depends on its parents for its healthy growth and a secure life in a family. It could be a one-parent family or a two-parent one. My father spent his childhood in a no-parent situation, which left an indelible impression on him for the rest of his life. I have observed a rare expression in his eyes, when a young mother was around holding her baby. I believe that the mother is the only true relative of the child and the role of the father is secondary. In an engineering sense, it is better to have a beam with two supports than only one built-in support, like a canopy or cantilever. The built-in support has to be specially strong, like a single mother. This model can work, although a two-parent family is a better balanced system. On the other hand, an adoring granny or a strong-minded aunt could create additional props, which could cause a loss of balance in the family environment. In some two-parent cases, the mother is still the built-in support and she takes most of the strain, while the father may serve just as a prop. He may be nearly ineffective as far as the development of a child is concerned, which has been the case during my own childhood.

Development of a child during its teenage years may depend purely on chance. A lot depends on the mother's earlier input but only a few youngsters are fortunate to meet the best persons in the right circumstances. For example, my uncle Hari met Mr Bailey at the right time. Some get the help and support from strange quarters. For instance, my life would have been different if I had not met Sulu and my lady teacher earlier and later, Dadaji, Mirzasaab and Angela. For many parents, teenagers develop as if they go on the other side of the moon, until they reappear later into some recognisable form! All the parents can do is to watch, and worry perhaps, and stand by in case something seems to be really disturbing.

Here I find something odd with the present day state of children in Asian families in the UK. We were not rich in Mumbai and we did not have all uniformly supportive relatives and neighbours. But we had some choice. Here, the choice is to stick with other Asian youngsters or to mix with the host community children, which happens in schools anyway.

I have found it despicable that some educated British parents should bring up their children with disrespect to other communities. It is possible that the ethnic minority adults are able to ignore and avoid the consequences of this attitude. I have noticed on some occasions that a seat next to an Asian, on a bus or train, would remain vacant. This is irrespective of the fact that Asians are most likely to be clean and tidy, as many of them bathe every day. All the same, some people would prefer to stand instead of sitting next to an Asian. I often joke that it is all right since the bus companies do not hold Asians responsible for such vacant seats and charge them double fare. Such tendencies of some people would hurt me a little but they must have a serious and undesirable effect on the children's attitude to the society, of which they are meant to become a part in the future.

Children are sensitive and youngsters have a natural tendency to group together and identify themselves with the majority section of their peers. Even to the mild consternation of their parents, Asian children like to speak only English, enjoy Western music and play the same games as their classmates. However, if this natural tendency does not receive a reciprocal response, an Asian child may find itself left out and could have some scars that may not heal. I have found that girls are also unkind to girls from other communities and even cruel at times. Some teachers tend to be less than generous and an Asian child might suffer from the feeling of antipathy from a source that is really meant to nurture a young mind and provide support during its formative years. Of course, no laws can change this and the situation may improve with time.

At the same time, many well-to-do Asian parents discourage their children from having white friends and they prefer to live near Asian strongholds, which will continue to worsen the situation in the long term. They should realise that they must participate in community life as much as possible. This is the only route to change the stereo-type impressions about Asians, given by the old stories and plays. Asians could be either Maharajahs, who must be all right anyway, or ignorant labourers, who could be a liability for the country. I have heard the most discerning local people remark that, as long as the Asians have some jobs, all problems should be considered as solved. This is not all right for the second generation Asians or those who came to the UK from the middle class environment. They have aspirations to do better and an urge to demonstrate their abilities, for their own good and for the sake of their children. The change can be brought about only over a long time and not through any law or Equal Opportunity Policy.

Nowadays, most youngsters are nurtured by a monster called the Media, mainly the television, and weaned on what is known as pop music. Not many children are fortunate enough to watch quality programmes or to listen to classical music. Most youngsters are exposed to the eardrum-shattering variety, without any lyric worth the name and with at the best three or four notes repeating over and over again.

It is unfortunate that some so-called funny TV programmes should have only the cheap variety of humour. TV could be as dangerous as a drug, when doses of sit-coms are administered to glamorise bad behaviour of men and to demean disciplined and studious youngsters in an absolutely ridiculous manner. Sustained influence of this treatment could destroy faith and belief in hard work and serious studies during the formative years of children.

The TV companies might consider making and showing programmes with a realistic representation of the bravery of commonwealth and Indian soldiers during the second world war. In most films, a coloured character is most likely to be killed well before the end of the film, when the white soldiers would be receiving the credit for their heroism. Programmes like "It ain't half hot mum" depict Indians as crazy orderlies or tea-boys, which could give a wrong impression of the role played by Indians in the war. This could not do any good to the morale of second generation Indians in the UK. They should know about the part played by their ancestors in saving the world from dictators. Such transmission of knowledge through the powerful means like television could give them the self-respect to make them feel like a legitimate part of the modern Western world.

Food habits symbolise another issue that seems to alienate Indians from the West. Although I am not a vegetarian, I am often misunderstood to be one because I am an Indian by birth. Many Indians eat meat like I do. But the popular image of an Indian is that of a vegetarian, who is supposed to have a calm temperament, a stereo-type attribute of vegetarianism. Some of my characters, including my mentor Dadaji, were vegetarians. I personally do not see any great merit in eating only rice and vegetables. It was all right when we did not know about plant-life or about the microscopic organisms we inhale or carry in our bodies all the time. The truth of the matter is that some lives have to end, if other lives are to be sustained. Geeta has verses to this effect. Vegetarians claim that the meat-proteins are undesirable for the health of the mind. I can accept that an excess of meat-proteins is bad but this can be said about anything taken in excess. Hindu tradition of meat-less days in a week would be ideal for keeping the balance. But the merits of vegetarianism in maintaining mental health and pious nature should not be overstated. Both Doctor and Manoj were vegetarians but they were not really pious and calm by nature. The link with vegetarianism and peacefulness must also be quite tentative. Have there been no psychopathic villains among vegetarian people?

However, the truth in the principle, "extinction of a life for sustaining another life", could become quite uncomfortable in the end, with a build-up of a worsening series of arguments. The next step in the natural progression is the axiom "survival of the fittest". Our ancestors cut down the trees that could not retaliate and which were provided by nature, free of cost. The human-beings proved to be fitter than others in the survival race, by developing weapons that could kill a number of animal species to extinction.

It was perhaps all right to kill an animal for food, as the Maoris and other tribal people did. But the religious rules should not have been written to justify the slaughter of animals. It must be a fallacy to say that only the human-being has a soul and an animal does not, and hence it can be killed. This is convenient but, like a bad clause in an engineering code of practice, it could lead to some dangerous interpretations.

Such add-on rules to religious practice have condoned atrocious acts like stuffing paste of corn in the throat of a goose to increase the size of its liver. Similarly, these rules permit farms keeping animals confined to small enclosures all their lives. If an animal lives under such circumstances, its body might produce enzymes as a result of the stressful condition of its mind, making the meat harmful to the consumer. We have not yet found this out but we know the horrors of the "mad-cow disease", resulting from feeding cows with animal products, instead of grass.

In the past, the religious licence to kill soul-less animals might have been extended to the humans belonging to other faith. Black Africans were not Christians and, in their jungle habitat, they couldn't have looked much like human-beings in the eyes of the European slave traders. In South America, the Spanish Conquistadors destroyed the natives by millions, with some similar support of the fabricated religious doctrines. Was all this all right? Even in India, the God himself, Lord Krishna, had a hand in destroying the Nagas, who were presumably human-beings but called serpents for the sake of convenience. The same logic applied in the following centuries, when the natives were converted and made lower caste servants, or killed if they resisted, by all those who invaded India until the British came to rule.

The bad situation becomes much worse when human injustice is justified as a religious act through the add-on doctrines. Such ungodly acts range from the deceitful "bread in the wells" conversion of ignorant people by the sixteenth century Portuguese missionaries to the tragedies at the time of partition of India in 1947.

Man's inhumanity towards man has plagued the human race for centuries. Hindus believe that the God Vishnu is born in the world to restore the balance between the good and the bad, like Buddha for example. Even Jesus Christ is regarded by some Hindus as one of the God's messengers. These corrective measures have sought to arrest the human tendency to curl away from a straight path. However, such tendency must be the singularly most important reason for miseries and an obstacle to continuous progress of the mankind.

One of the most undesirable by-product of historical acts of man's inhumanity towards other men is to make many people lose faith in God and religion. We often hear that, if God really existed, He should have prevented the injustice. However, many people I have really respected for different reasons, uncle Hari, Dadaji, Mirzasaab and Macalister, were believers. On the other hand, I have read about some intellectual non-believers, who are really godly people in my opinion, for example, Lord Bertrand Russell and Harold Hardy, the Cambridge mathematician. Hardy has even admitted that the happiest hours of his life were spent within sound of a Roman Catholic Church! This experience relates to Hardy's time at Fenner's, when the chimes of six o'clock fell across the ground on quiet and lovely evenings in May! Such musical sounds in those surroundings could also have reminded a devout Hindu of God's existence.

In ordinary life, people do not believe in God as a protest against the crimes carried out in the name of religion or a sect of religion. The former Yugoslavia is a case in point. Again, it is not correct to say that a certain religion is the best because the original scriptures say everything that is good. Jainism has one of the strictest principles of behaviour. However, Doctor, Manoj and many other businessmen in Mumbai may not be the examples for proving the point that Jainism is the most ideal religion. A religion should be tested on the basis of the behaviour of people who belong to the religion. It must sound ironical, therefore, that some religions do not encourage the followers to criticise the Scriptures and their doctrines do not allow the question "why?", when the religious leaders expect the followers to do something that is seemingly wrong.

Learning is one of the ways of worship in Hindu religion, which primarily advocates seeking an answer to the question "why?". The main religious Hindu book, Geeta, is really a record of religious discussion, questions and answers. This tradition was carried on and criticism and review have been the subjects of many subsequent religious books.

The questions "When?", "Where?" and "How?" can be answered through reading what is available and memorising it without understanding the essence of the subject. This way, one can give an impression of having achieved something and for many commercial functions, this is adequate. In effect, some religious establishments forbid the question "Why?", to avoid explanations to anomalies created by departure from basic principles and to promote political and commercial practices under the banner of the religion.

A thinking follower of a religion may come across a common conflict in the form of changes in the present and the past brought about by the advance of science and technology. This is why Galileo had to suffer a few centuries ago, when he expressed his belief that the earth went round the sun. More generally, the knowledge has widened in addition to its deepening, compared with that in the beginning of the first millennium. Men at the helm of Christianity, one of the tolerant regions, must have decided against trying to understand other theologies, even when they knew about their existence. They might have just pulled the shutters down and declared that there could be "no other God" and the only way to the God had to be through Jesus Christ. My mother-in-law and Macalister, both devout Christians, did not approve of such narrow interpretation of religious principles. However, the Christian priests must have taken the view that by declaring singularity of the "Son of God", they could be the next order relations of God. They could then maintain authority over the masses. This would have ensured religious discipline and a sound and coherent structure to the religion. Furthermore, it must have been convenient to encourage learning of the Scriptures only that could compliment the central rule of the Church and the establishment.

Many Indians have admired the character of Jesus and treated him at par with the other messengers of God. This is one of the beautiful aspects of pantheism. A businessman could be a devotee of Laxmi, the goddess of wealth, and an intellectual could worship Saraswati, the goddess of learning. Why could the omnipresent, omniscient and omnipotent God not present different gifts to different human beings in various places, and send His sons and daughters to guide them further?

People from different religions have added to my own concept of faith and way of life. In reality, I was closer to the sound thinking of Mirzasaab than my uncle Hari's adherence to prescriptive rules, in religion and in engineering. Many lessons could be learnt from the behaviour of people who practised Hindu religion, which was apparently tarnished during the nineteenth and twentieth centuries. It should have received some polish to reveal that it did not follow the basic principles given in Geeta. Indians had probably gone too soft and lost the steely backbone of discipline and belief in their past. I could give some examples, large and small; handing over of their States to the British by Indian rulers without any will to resist, lack of long-term vision of my ancestors in losing their properties and land, Nanaji's reverence coupled with the weakness in his character, Mr Juhukar's lack of practical judgement and preference to uphold theoretical principles, etc.

Perhaps Hindus could learn a degree of discipline from Christians and Muslims, without compromising with their pantheist principles. On the other hand, Christianity could extend its tolerance to the acceptance of other faiths and "children of God". Such a combination could then enable spreading belief in the divinity all over the world, through logical and common principles and without any imposed and artificial expressions of mutual intolerance.

Interaction between religions is a desirable thing. The UK has the unique and advantageous position, gained through the historical background of the country. Millions of people all over the world, with various religious and cultural backgrounds, know and admire British literature, political system and the progressiveness of the people regarding religion. More important, people of different faith have come together here and they are less sensitive to the old differences between their cultures and religions. In many parts of the world, the newcomers have influenced the local people but in a violent manner. In the UK, there is a chance of peaceful evolution of tolerant religious philosophies, which could challenge the add-on, prescriptive and ungodly practices in individual cases. I could almost visualise a situation, vaguely similar to that of my ancestors, who came to Mumbai from Rajputana in northern India and formed alliance with the local people. One would wish that such agreeable meetings of cultures could have occurred in many other parts of the world. However, history tells you as things happened and may not necessarily teach any lessons!

There are some signs that religious authorities may change their attitude towards the influence of science on some outdated, rigid, unrealistic and divisive principles. I have mentioned the injustice done to Galileo by the Vatican in the seventeenth century. The astronomer was found guilty of heresy, based on some fabricated evidence, and put under house arrest for the last eight years of his life in Florence. The Church considered that Galileo had expressed views in favour of the Copernican Sun-centred system, as opposed to the Ptolemic Earth-centred universe, in his work *Dialogue concerning the Two Chief World Systems.* Some three hundred and fifty-five years later, the Pope, Head of the Roman Catholic Church, has quoted from Galileo in his thirteenth encyclical, *Fides et Ratio,* as reported in the press in mid-October 98. The Pontiff had previously admitted that the Church was wrong to treat the astronomer as it did, but it is quite extraordinary for the Pope to quote faith and science as the two truths and that they cannot contradict each other. The Pope has used his strongest words against theologians who ignore philosophy and quoted the Second Vatican Council as saying,

"Methodical research, in all realms of knowledge, if it respects moral norms, will never be genuinely opposed to faith."

One cannot expect the Pope to be more explicit than what he has said. However, he is known to have favoured exploring the *why of things* in full harmony of the search for the ultimate answer, which could enable human reason to reach its zenith and to open to the religious impulse. The Pope has also pointed out that the Church may seem negative about ideas and that it should encourage philosophical enquiry. It is tempting to visualise that, in this Papal plea for union of reason and faith, there may be seeds for evolution leading to a pragmatic religion.

I believe firmly that children would benefit from such pragmatic religion. They should have an input of renovated religious principles during their development in adulthood, which would not suffocate their desire to learn. Not everyone would be naturally gifted like Lord Russell and Harold Hardy, who could do without any such support. A child has a natural tendency to belong to someone and adore something, its own mother or a friend or anything else. In the absence of a proper model with positive attributes, young minds are attracted to the superficial glitz of pop-stars and footballers. This tendency is unfortunately and mercilessly exploited by commercial agents. On the other hand, young people are likely to hate leaders of society, because of the media publicity of corrupt politicians, wanton heads of states and errant priests. In the earlier days, kings and queens could have provided models with real and regal skills acquired through strict self-discipline and upbringing. I believe that this was one of the sources of strength for the British people and their empire.

In my opinion, we should accept inadequacies and imperfection of human life and look upon God as an abstract Universal phenomenon. There is no place in the modern world for warped theologies departing from basic principles, illogical and outmoded doctrines and ill-disciplined and weak religions. Models of godliness need not even be kept in the confined spaces like churches, temples and mosques, but they should be brought out in the open spaces, lakes and riversides. This way, a modern and moderate Harold Hardy may find his happy moments in such godly places, without treating God as his personal enemy!.

The symbols of Godliness are in abundance in nature, blooming flowers, the sunrise, the sunset, etc. Pleasures from music, sculpture, literature and sciences make life worth living for its little surprises and promote hard work and healthy competition. One must not be despondent because some things could not be found or understood precisely. One should not lose faith if the world is not what it could have been. Apart from the God's abstractness, the concept of Him giving the direction is the most useful one in practice. "Remember me and compete" is the best message of God that should keep us going, no matter what stories we believe in or what our background may be. Many people, like Mirzasaab, Eric and I, could find common grounds in their lives, in spite of their different backgrounds and religions.

The stories and the recorded experience of one's ancestors are indispensable parts of human history. However, they should be seen as a record and not tablets of stone. Religious doctrines should be regularly questioned and reviewed, to keep them in harmony with the state of modern development. Such progressive religion may provide a haven for some vulnerable section of the future generation. Otherwise it could drift like a rudderless ship, into some treacherous waters of declining standards, drugs and decadence.

If no one cares, the desire for money and material pleasures will conquer and rule, and the process may become irreversible. The spirit of sport and music is slowly but surely being weakened in this way. This might be followed by commercialisation of other arts and education and no one knows what will happen to the human race in the next millennium. Like the loss of forests in the olden days and the extinction of species through mindless killing of animals, the villainous tendency will prevail over the godly nature of mankind. Man's inhumanity will know no bounds, if there is no counterbalancing reaction through a revival of realistic religious principles. The only hope to arrest the sliding down of humanity towards the precipice is through an evolution leading to a progressive religion and rejuvenation of faith in the universal God. I hope that the good words expressed in the encyclical by His Holiness the Pope lead to such evolution in the future.